LANDSCAPES OF
MADEIRA
a countryside guide

*Third edition,
revised and enlarged*

John and Pat Underwood

SUNFLOWER
BOOKS

Dedicated to

'Mr Joseph'—Sr José Fernandes
Head Porter at Reid's Hotel

who urged us to see more of his island
and so quite changed our lives!

Copyright © 1988
Sunflower Books
12 Kendrick Mews
London SW7 3HG, UK

First published 1980
Second edition 1983

ISBN: 0 948513 22 5

IMPORTANT NOTE TO THE READER ━━━━━━━━

We have tried to ensure that the descriptions and maps in this book are as accurate as possible as we go to press. Unfortunately, major roadworks are in progress all over the island. Many walks are affected; several descriptions are very likely to be out of date — simply because conditions are changing from day to day. If you find your walk or tour affected by roadworks, *do* have a word with the builders. Name your destination; if they have provided a new route, they will point it out to you. Equally, if the way is impassable for the present time, they will let you know, even if by sign language. **DO refer to the STOP PRESS entries.**

While we visit Madeira regularly, we also rely on your help to keep the book up to date. Any corrections or suggestions will be gratefully received and incorporated, where necessary, into future printings. We also rely on walkers to take along a good supply of common sense when they ramble on Madeira. **At any time**, new construction or storm damage may alter the course of a walk and make it unsafe. If the route is not as we outline it, and your way ahead is not secure, return to the safe point of departure. **Do not attempt to complete a walk under hazardous conditions.** Please read pages 34—41 carefully and heed our warnings to walk *safely*, while at the same time respecting the beauty of the countryside.
— Pat and John Underwood

Photographs by John Underwood
Maps by Pat Underwood
Drawings by Katharina Kelly
Typeset by Allset Composition, London
Colour origination by Duplichrome Ltd, Birmingham
Printed and bound in the UK by A Wheaton and Co Ltd, Exeter
B/BH

 Contents

Foreword/João Carlos Abreu   5

Preface to the third edition   6
  Levadas — Acknowledgements — Books   6

Getting about   9
  Map of Funchal centre   10
    city exits · petrol stations · bus stops
  Where to find your bus   10

Picnicking   12
  Picnic suggestions   13

Touring   17
  EASTERN MADEIRA'S GENTLE CHARMS (TOUR 1)   18
    Palheiro Gardens · Camacha · Santo da Serra · Ponta de
    São Lourenço · Machico · Santa Cruz · Garajau · Funchal

  THE CORRAL AND THE CAPE (TOUR 2)   21
    Pico dos Barcelos · Eira do Serrado · Curral das Freiras ·
    Câmara de Lobos · Cabo Girão · (Optional: Jardim da
    Serra) · Funchal

  MOUNTAINS AND MORE MOUNTAINS! (TOUR 3)   23
    Terreiro da Luta · Poiso · Arieiro · Portela · Porto da
    Cruz · Faial · Santana · Achada do Teixeira · Ribeiro
    Frio · Funchal

  MADEIRA NORTH AND SOUTH (TOUR 4)   27
    Ribeira Brava · Encumeada · São Vicente · Boaventura ·
    Santana · Faial · Ribeiro Frio · Poiso · Monte · Funchal

  PORTO MONIZ AND PAÚL DA SERRA (TOUR 5)   30
    Ribeira Brava · São Vicente · Seixal · Porto Moniz ·
    Ribeira da Janela Valley · Paúl da Serra · Canhas · Funchal

  THE SUNNY SOUTHWEST COAST (TOUR 6)   33
    Ribeira Brava · Canhas · Arco da Calheta · Prazeres · Ponta
    do Pargo · Ribeira da Janela Valley · Paúl da Serra · Funchal

Walking   34
  Guides, waymarking, maps   34
  Walkers' checklist   35
  Where to stay   36
  Weather   36
  What to take   38
  Portuguese for walkers   39
  A country code for walkers and motorists   40
  Organisation of the walks   41
  The walks (see overleaf)   42

FUNCHAL AND THE SOUTHEAST

1 Funchal · Socorridos River (Levada dos Piornais) Vitória 42
2 Curral das Freiras · Fajã · Funchal (Levada do Curral e Castelejo) 44
3 Corticeiras · Boca dos Namorados · Curral das Freiras 51
4 Corticeiras · Pico Grande · Encumeada (or Curral) 52
5 Candelária · Tábua · Corujeira (Levada Nova) · Ribeira Brava 56
6 Estreito de Câmara de Lobos · Quinta Grande · Campanário · Boa Morte (Levada do Norte) · Barreiras 58
7 Babosas · Palheiro Ferreiro · Lombo Grande (Levada dos Tornos) · Gaula 63
8 Camacha · Salgados · Assomada (Levada do Caniço) 67
9 Terreiro da Luta · Monte · Choupana · Camacha (Levada dos Tornos and Levada da Serra) 69
10 Camacha · João Frino · Santo da Serra (Levada da Serra 72
11 Exploring São Lourenço Point 75
12 Portela to Pico do Facho (Levada Machico—Caniçal) 78

THE NORTHEAST AND THE GREAT PEAKS

13 The north coast path: Ribeira Sêca · Boca do Risco · Porto da Cruz 82
14 Queimadas · Levada do Caldeirão Verde · Santana 87
15 Achada do Teixeira · Pico Ruivo · Torrinhas Pass · Encumeada 89
16 Achada do Teixeira · Pico Ruivo · Torrinhas Pass · Curral das Freiras 93
17 Pico das Pedras · Cova da Roda · Lombo do Galego · Cruzinhas (or Faial) 94
18 The high peaks: Pico do Arieiro · Pico Ruivo · Queimadas · Santana 96
19 Ribeiro Frio · Lamaceiros · Portela (Levada do Furado and Levada da Portela) 99
20 Encumeada · Ginjas waterhouse (Levada do Norte) · Feiteiras 101
21 Encumeada · Pico Redondo · Pousada dos Vinháticos 105
22 Encumeada · Cascalho · Encumeada (Levada do Norte and Levada das Rabaças) 106
23 Encumeada · Pináculo · Caramujo · Ginjas waterhouse · Feiteiras (or Encumeada) 108
24 Encumeada · Levada do Lombo do Mouro · Ribeira Brava 111

THE WEST AND NORTHWEST

25 A ramble round Prazeres 112
26 Campo Grande · Rabaçal · Loreto 114
27 Paúl da Serra · Fanal · Ribeira da Janela 121
28 Rabaçal · Risco · 25 Fontes · Rabaçal 124

Touring map *between pages* 16 and 17
Bus timetables 126
Index of geographical names 133
    Pronunciation/translation of some index entries 135
STOP PRESS 135

◉ Foreword

To visit Madeira — at any time of the year — and not to go on foot along the island's paths and trails, up to the mountain crests and ever closer to heaven, is to miss seeing and 'feeling' the island in its full majesty. To know Madeira, we have to cross it with the levadas, listening to the hymn of their waters. We have to experience the sacred silence of the summits. Up there, beside the 'Man on Foot', lost in a veritable sea of clouds, the walker establishes that paradisial rapport that man can — at times — have with nature.

We Madeirans know that the cascade of the waters, the breath of the flowers, the murmur of the trees, the surge of the springs are the life force of our island, making it a true paradise afloat in the Atlantic. Our earth is impregnated with the sweat and the love of generation upon generation of our people who were born and who died here, carrying out their gigantic life's work of transforming the land into terraces reaching from the sea far up the mountainsides — people who wrote with their souls a true epic, which can only be 'read' and understood by those who tread in their footsteps along the mountain paths.

So we welcome with delight publication of this new edition of *Landscapes of Madeira*: this excellent book is the ideal companion for those who wish to have an authentic experience of our island, with its unending panoramas of majesty and poetry. John and Pat Underwood know the deep secrets of Madeira: through their long and continuous walking they have penetrated the island as few others have, and they have brought their understanding to the publication of this work. This indispensable guide will help everyone who uses it to discover the enchantments of our land. Our deep thanks and best wishes to John and Pat for their contribution to the tourism of Madeira — an island that welcomes you with the warmth and brotherhood of its people and the exuberance and friendship of its landscapes.

JOÃO CARLOS ABREU
Secretary of Culture and Tourism

☀ Preface

Since we first published a small book of Madeira walks in 1980, not only has *Landscapes of Madeira* become by far the most widely-used guide to the island, but it inspired a whole series of 'Landscapes' books, which we publish under our Sunflower imprint.

The aim of the series is to give tourists what João Carlos Abreu, in his Foreword, calls 'an authentic experience of the island'. Each 'Landscape' guide is written by someone who knows the terrain intimately and who hopes to lead the visitor off the beaten track and into the countryside — whether by car, public transport, or on foot.

This third edition of *Landscapes of Madeira* includes several new walks; in fact, you can now cross the island on footpaths, using our notes. And we've included more information for walkers travelling by car. However, the emphasis is on *presentation*. All the maps have been re-drawn; all are in colour. Many new photographs are included.

All the Sunflower authors hope to convey more than mere enthusiasm for their chosen landscapes — love might be a better word. Our love affair with Madeira really came into blossom with our 'discovery' of the levadas. They have never ceased to fascinate or inspire us. No matter how tired we may be, to walk beside a levada always refreshes our spirits and brings the bounce back into our steps.

The Levadas

Whether you use the book to tour, walk or picnic, we will lead you along the *levadas*. These watercourses are not unique to Madeira: what *is* unique is their **accessibility** and **extent**. You need only venture a little way off the main roads to begin to appreciate Madeira's myriad aqueducts — for their beauty, ingenuity of design, and for the courage and deter-mination needed to bring the concept to its present glory. The island's irrigation system now comprises an impressive 2150km/1333mi of channels, including 40km/25mi of tunnels — and the work started centuries ago.

The earliest settlers on Madeira began cultivating the lower slopes in the south of the island, cutting out *poios* (terraces). Working with contractors (who sometimes used slave or convict labour), they built the first small levadas, which carried water from springs higher up the mountainsides to irrigate their lands. The first legislation dealing with levadas and water rights dates back to the second half of the fifteenth century.

By the early 1900s, there were about 200 of these levadas, meandering over about 1000km/620mi. Many were privately owned, and the undisciplined appropriation of water meant that the island's most valuable asset was often unfairly distributed. In fact, by the mid-1930s, only two-thirds of the island's arable land was under cultivation — and just half of that was irrigated. Only the State had the money to implement a major building programme and the authority to enforce a more equitable system of distribution.

For there was plenty of water for irrigation, and torrents to spare for power! Clouds driven to the island by the prevailing northeast winds are caught by the central mountain chain, and as much as 2m/80in of rain may fall in the north in a year — while the south coast may be dry for up to six months. It is said that the island is a huge self-regulating reservoir, holding up to 200 million cubic metres — 44,000 million gallons — of water, for the rain seeps down into porous volcanic ash. Soon it meets layers of basaltic clay and laterite — both quite impervious. Here the water wells up again in springs, and if not channelled, pours untapped — as it has for centuries — down countless ravines, into the sea.

In 1939 the Portuguese government sent a mission to the island to study a combined irrigation/hydroelectric scheme. The 'new' levadas created from its plans are channelled out at an altitude of about 1000m/3300ft, where the concentra-

tion of rainfall, dew and springs is greatest. The water is conveyed first to power stations lying just at the outer edge of the arable land (about 600m/2000ft); then it flows on into the irrigated zones. Here, distribution is carried out by the *levadeiro*, who diverts the flow to each proprietor.

Most of the mission's development plans were implemented by 1970. Among the most important projects were the Levada do Norte and the Levada dos Tornos, both of which you will discover as you tour, walk or picnic. Their incredible length, considering the terrain, is best gauged on the large colour map. You will marvel that the job could have been accomplished in so short a time, for all the work was done by hand. How were the tunnels cut through the solid basalt? How did the workers channel out the levadas under the icy-cascading waterfalls, halfway between earth and sky? Often, as was the case with the construction of the corniche road between São Vicente and Porto Moniz, they were suspended from above, in wicker baskets, while they fought the unyielding stone with picks. Many lost their lives to bring water and electricity to the islanders and unending joy to those who 'listen to the hymn of their waters'.

Acknowledgements

We are very grateful for the invaluable help of the following:

For guiding: Luis de Sousa and John Blandy;

For help with maps and plans: The Regional Government of Madeira, especially Eng Leandro Câmara, Eng Jorge Jardim Fernandes and Eng Felipe Ferreira; and the Instituto Geográfico e Cadastral, for permission to adapt their maps;

For checking the walks: It would be impossible to name all the people who have contributed corrections and suggestions for this new edition; we have received hundreds of letters since the second edition was published. Please continue to send your comments; they are helpful to everyone who uses the book. Special thanks, however, to Clive Scott, who did most of the walks in the book, and George Watt, who accompanied us prior to publication of this edition.

For support and encouragement: The Madeira Tourist Office in Funchal, especially João Carlos Abreu, Secretary of Culture and Tourism, for his Foreword; and the Portuguese National Tourist Office in London.

Books

The *definitive* guide to Madeira's flora is **Madeira: Plants and Flowers** (Franquinho and da Costa, 1986). All the walks and car tours in this book are cross-referenced to our own picture book, **Madeira** (1987 edition), to inspire you in advance and make a lasting souvenir. Both **Madeira** and **Madeira: Plants and Flowers** are available on the island. They may also be ordered in advance from your local bookseller or Sunflower Books.

☀ Getting about

There is no doubt that a **hired car** or taxi is the most convenient way of getting round the island, and if four people are sharing the cost it becomes an attractive idea — especially for journeys to the north and west. We hope that the liberal cross-references to picnics and walks in the touring section will inspire motorists and walkers to team up on car hire. *New in this third edition:* all the walking maps show the car symbol (🚗) wherever you may park near the path of a walk.

There is a fixed rate for all **taxi journeys** outside the city: a price list is available at the Tourist Office, or your hotel porter may have a copy. Your hotel porter may also be able to suggest a particular driver for your all-day tour: some are especially knowledgeable; a few are keen walkers too!

Coach tours are the most popular way of 'seeing Madeira in a day'. They provide a painless introduction to road conditions and a remarkable overview of island scenery. You'll discover in comfort the landscapes you'll want to explore at leisure, on your own.

Our favourite way of getting about is by **local bus**. The system is very economical, reliable, and fun! You get splendid views perched up on bus seats, and most of the buses making long journeys are new and quite comfortable. The map on the following pages shows you where to board your bus in Funchal, and where to purchase tickets. (Note that, outside the capital, you can flag down a bus anywhere along its route, without making for the centre of a village.)

Please do not rely *solely* on the bus departure times given in this book: changes are fairly frequent. The Tourist Office sells a **bus timetable** at a nominal charge, but even this is not always up to date. It's best to visit the bus kiosks in Funchal (see map page 10), where the latest schedules are posted. Don't be confused, either, by similar bus numbers. Some 'town' buses (orange) have the same numbers as country buses (eg orange town bus 20 to Monte; green/cream country bus 20 to Santo da Serra). *It always pays to verify bus departures and seat availability* for long journeys; this can also be done at the kiosks. *And it is best to arrive well before departure time.* In Funchal's 'sea' of buses, it may take you several minutes to find the one you want. Also, in our experience, buses leave exactly on time — or a minute or two early!

LEGEND

1	Tourist Office	20	Municipal Museum
2	Statue of Zarco	21	Post Office
3	Blandy Agency (British Consulate)	22	São Lourenço Palace
4	Air Portugal	23	Colegiate Church
5	Municipal Theatre	24	Museum of Wine
6	Casa do Turista	25	Law Courts
7	Government Offices	26	Town Hall
8	Sé Cathedral	27	Sacred Art Museum
9	Old Customs House	28	New Customs House
10	Infante Fountains	29	Market
11	Statue of Henry the Navigator	30	Forte de São Tiago
12	Santa Caterina Chapel	31	Old Town
13	President's House	32	Boat Trips
14	Casino	33	Corpo Santo
15	Hospital	34	Santa Maria Major
16	Barreiros Stadium	35	Carmo
17	Forte do Pico	36	Bom Jesus
18	Quinta das Cruzes	37	Incarnation
19	Santa Clara Convent	38	St John's
		39	St Peter's
		40	St Paul's

🚕 Taxis   ⛽ Petrol Stations

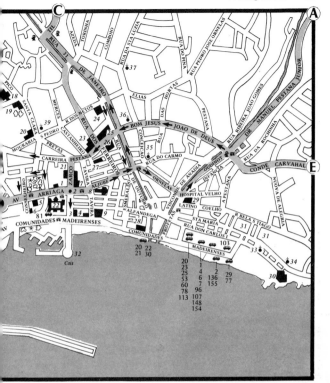

🚌 No.	Colour	Final Destination	Departure Point
1	cream/red	Ponta dos Frades	'Bus Station', seafront
2	red/grey	Assomada	east end of seafront
4	cream/red	Ponta do Sol	'Bus Station', seafront
6	cream/red	Boaventura	'Bus Station', seafront
7	cream/red	Ribeira Brava	'Bus Station', seafront
20	cream/green	Santo da Serra	'Bus Station', seafront
20, 21	white/blue/green*	Monte	opposite the new customs house
22	as 20, 21	Babosas	as 20, 21
23	cream/green	Machico	'Bus Station', seafront
25	cream/green	Santo da Serra	'Bus Station', seafront
29	cream/blue	Camacha	east end of seafront
30, 37	white/blue/green	Babosas, Botanical Gardens	seafront, opposite Rua Profetas
53	cream/green	Faial, Igreja	'Bus Station', seafront
60	cream/green	Boqueirão	'Bus Station', seafront
77	cream/blue	Santo da Serra	east end of seafront
78	cream/green	Faial via Machico	'Bus Station', seafront
81	cream/blue	Curral das Freiras	west of Casa do Turista
96	cream/red	Corticeiras	'Bus Station', seafront
103	grey/red	Boaventura	'Bus Station', east end
107	cream/red	Raposeira	'Bus Station', seafront
113	cream/green	Caniçal	'Bus Station', seafront
136	red/grey	Vargem	east end of seafront
148	cream/red	Boa Morte	'Bus Station', seafront
154	cream/red	Cabo Girão	'Bus Station', seafront
155	red/grey	Ponta da Oliveira	east end of seafront

*These will soon be orange

✸ Picnicking

A day's outing centred round a picnic that you've gathered together at the early morning market is a holiday treat that you'll treasure in memory for many months to come, and it's so easy: you can get to your picnic by bus, car or taxi. Choose one of the established picnic sites with tables (most are on main roads and are indicated in our touring notes and on the touring map by the **x** symbol), or find a more secluded spot along the path of a walk.

All the information you need to get to these 'private' picnics is given on pages 13–16, where *picnic numbers correspond to walk numbers*, so that you can quickly find the general location on the island by looking at the touring map. Unfortunately, not every walk boasts an easy-to-reach picnic spot: for instance, we suggest two picnics along the path of Walk 6, but none for Walks 2, 3 or 5, etc. We give you walking times, transport details (🚌 = bus numbers, 🚗 = car or taxi parking) and map references. The location of the picnic is indicated by the symbol *P* on the appropriate *walking map*, which also shows 🚌 and 🚗 locations.

Please remember that these picnic suggestions are 'off the beaten track': you will want to wear sensible shoes **and take a sunhat** (the symbol ○ at the left of the picnic number reminds you that the picnic is **in full sun**). It's a good idea to take along a plastic groundsheet as well.

To choose a spot that appeals to you, photograph references are given for each picnic suggestion. If you're just flipping through the book and you see a landscape that appeals, the photograph caption will tell you if this picture is of one of our 'private' picnic spots and will indicate the picnic number.

If you are travelling to your picnic by bus, be sure to check our bus timetables with the latest schedules shown in the kiosks in Funchal (see 'Getting about', page 9). **If you are travelling to your picnic by taxi from your hotel**, and you want the taxi driver to wait for you, it is customary to invite him to join in your picnic. **If you are travelling by car,** be extra vigilant off the main roads, where children and animals are not used to traffic. Without damaging plants, be sure to park *well off* the road; *never* block a road or track!

All picnickers should read the country code on page 40 and go quietly in the countryside.

1 SOCORRIDOS VALLEY (map page 45; photograph page 43)

by car or taxi: 8–10min on foot   *by bus: 8–10min on foot*
🚗Lombada: Take the northbound road at Vitória (1km east of Câmara de Lobos, signposted 'Pico dos Barcelos') to Lombada 0.7km north
🚌 1 or 3 to Lombada (departs from front of São Lourenço Palace); these orange 'town' buses run frequently; check times at kiosk

From Lombada, go northwest up the cobbled road and immediately fork right up cobbled 'steps' to climb to the Levada dos Piornais (4min). Turn left; the valley overlook is reached in five minutes more. There are two narrow places along the levada (drops of 7m/20ft) on one side only

○4 BOCA DA CORRIDA (map page 54; photograph page 53)

by car or taxi: 0–10min on foot   *by bus and taxi: 0–10min*
🚗Boca da Corrida: From Estreito de Câmara de Lobos, take the northbound road signposted 'Jardim da Serra'. Beyond Corticeiras the road deteriorates somewhat as it passes the Quinta do Jardim da Serra to climb to Boca da Corrida
🚌 4, 6, 7, 96 or 107 to Estreito de Câmara de Lobos and *taxi from Estreito to Boca da Corrida*

Picnic just at the end of the road, or – better by far – use notes on page 52 (last paragraph) to start Walk 4

6a BOA MORTE'S PINES (map page 59; photograph page 61)

by car or taxi: 0–5min on foot   *by bus: 10–15min on foot*
🚗Boa Morte forest: Take road to Boa Morte (3km west of Campanario at the 172km marker – *not signposted*); follow road uphill to the Levada do Norte, where you can park on one of the tracks
🚌 148 to Boa Morte (see under 'Short walk 3', page 58): Walk up the *paved road* out of the village to levada in the forest (10–15min)

Picnic in pines anywhere along the levada

6b RIBEIRA BRAVA VALLEY (map page 59; photograph page 62)

by car or taxi: 15min on foot   *by bus: 15min on foot*
🚗as 6a above: Then walk west along the levada for fifteen minutes
🚌 148 to Boa Morte (see under 'Short walk 3', page 58): Walk up the *dirt track* west of the village to reach the levada; then turn left

An interesting contrast to the valley overlook of Picnic 1

7a BABOSAS BALCONY (map pages 70–71; photograph page 64)

by car or taxi: 0–10min on foot   *by bus: 0–10min on foot*
🚗Babosas Balcony: Take the EN103 to Monte, turning right to find Babosas (or park at Monte and walk to the viewpoint; see page 69)
🚌 20 or 21 to Monte or 🚌 22 to Babosas

The viewpoint (or 'balcony') overlooks Curral dos Romeiros; you can picnic on the stone 'seats' here, or start out on the path of Walk 7, going as far as you like – perhaps down to the bridge crossing the Ribeira de João Gomes. Our photograph is looking *towards*, not away from, the picnic setting

7b PORTO NOVO VALLEY (map pages 70—71, photograph page 75)

by car or taxi: 15—20min on foot   *by bus:15—20min on foot*

▣Levada dos Tornos reservoir: Follow northbound EN206 to Gaula, passing a church on the right after 3km. Turn left up a dirt track to the reservoir (easily seen from the road), just under 1km north of the church

🚌 60, signed 'Boqueirão'. Ask the driver for 'Levada dos Tornos, Lombo Grande'. From the bus stop, walk north up the EN206 for one minute to find the levada crossing. The 11.00 departure from Funchal (Mondays to Saturdays) and the 16.15 return make this a very convenient picnic

Turn left on the levada: ten minutes' walking will give you good views, or go as far as the 'window tunnel' described on page 66 (twenty minutes). This picnic affords an outlook over the *western* side of the Porto Novo Valley

8 PORTO NOVO VALLEY (map pages 70—71; photograph page 62)

by car or taxi: 15—20min on foot   *by bus: 25—30min on foot*

▣Assomada, on a dirt track: Turn north up the road on the east side of Assomada's church; bear left and *left again* to join the track passing an electricity sub-station (a squarish concrete building, easily seen from the main road). Pass the station and continue up to the *second* group of houses, where the track swings left. Park here; it's a three-minute walk up to the levada

🚌 2 to Assomada *church*, from where it's a 20min walk to levada

By bus or car, use the notes under 'Short walk 2' on page 67 to find the levada. Turn right on to the watercourse and find good picnicking spots (*eastern* outlook) in 5—10min

9 PARADISE VALLEY (map pages 70—71; photograph page 68)

by car or taxi: 2min on foot   *by bus: 6—8min on foot*

▣Levada da Serra: Take the EN203 (between Palheiro Ferreiro and Camacha) towards Poiso; it crosses the levada just past a restaurant. Park at the side of the road

🚌 29 or 77; ask for 'Restaurante, Vale do Paraíso'. From the bus stop, climb up the EN203 to find the levada just past the restaurant (about 5min)

Turn right on the levada and find the setting illustrated on page 68 in a few minutes

10 LEVADA DA SERRA (map pages 70—71; photograph page 74)

by car or taxi: 15min on foot   *by bus: 30min on foot*

▣Levada da Serra: The EN202 crosses the levada 0.5km west of the EN102 (between João Frino and Santo da Serra)

🚌 77; ask for 'Sitio das Quatro Estradas': From the bus stop, walk up the road signposted 'Arieiro' for 15min to reach the levada

Turn left on the levada: soon you will come to the archway of oaks shown in the photograph on page 74. Another good picnic spot is below the bridge over the João Frino River

○11 ABRA BAY (map page 77; photograph page 21)

by car or taxi: 0—5min on foot   *by bus and taxi: 0—5min*
🚌Abra Bay: The EN101-3 terminates here at a viewpoint
🚌 113 to Caniçal and *taxi to Abra Bay*
See page 76, third paragraph; walk as far as you like

○12 PICO DO FACHO (map page 81; no photograph)

by car or taxi: 5min on foot   *by bus: 30min on foot*
🚌Pico do Facho: The road is at the west side of the Caniçal tunnel
🚌 113; ask for 'Pico do Facho'. From the stop, it's a 25min climb
to the viewpoint
At the peak, five minutes' walking will lead to good picnic
spots away from the main viewpoint

14 QUEIMADAS (large-scale pull-out map; photograph page 86)

by car or taxi: 0—5min on foot   *by bus and taxi: 0—5min on foot*
🚌Queimadas Park, reached by a steep track *west* of Santana. Note
that even though the EN101-5 east of Santana is signposted to
both Pico Ruivo and Queimadas, you *cannot* drive to Queimadas
this way; you would have to park at Pico das Pedras and walk to
Queimadas (35min)
🚌 103 to Santana and *taxi to Queimadas*
Picnic at the rustic table by the pousada, or better still,
explore the surrounds (there are other picnic tables by the
levada track to Pico das Pedras)

○15 HOMEM EM PÉ (large-scale pull-out map; photograph page 88)

by car or taxi: 5—50min on foot   *by bus and taxi: 5—50min*
🚌Achada do Teixeira: The EN101-5 terminates here
🚌 103 to Santana and *taxi to Achada do Teixeira*
For full notes, see Walk 15 (starting on page 89). Picnic at
Homem em Pé or walk up to Pico Ruivo

17 COVA DA RODA (large-scale pull-out map; photograph page 86)

by car or taxi: 40min on foot   *by bus and taxi: 40min on foot*
🚌Pico das Pedras: Park 250m below forestry house on EN101-5
🚌 103 to Santana and *taxi to Pico das Pedras*
See 'Short walk 2' on page 94 to reach on of the island's
best viewpoints

○18 ARIEIRO (large-scale pull-out map; photograph page 97)

by car or taxi: 5—10min on foot   *by bus: not easily accessible*
🚌Arieiro: Take the EN202 from Poiso
Picnic near the start of Walk 18; notes on page 96

19a BALCÕES (large-scale pull-out map; photograph page 29)

by car or taxi: 20min on foot   *by bus: 20min on foot*
🚌Ribeiro Frio (EN103, north of Poiso)   🚌 103 to Ribeiro Frio
See notes at the foot of page 25 to walk to this wonderful
viewpoint

19b LAMACEIROS (map page 71; no photograph)

by car or taxi: 0–5min on foot   *by bus: not easily accessible*
🚗Lamaceiros, near the forestry house: The track (proposed EN203-1)
leads west off the EN102 south of Portela
The best picnic spot is just where the track meets the
levada; there are wonderful views of Penha de Águia

20 LAPA DO GALHO (large-scale pull-out map; photo page 26)

by car or taxi: 10–15min on foot   *by bus: 10–15min on foot*
🚗Encumeada, by the bar   🚌6 to Encumeada
Join the Levada do Norte a few steps up from the road,
opposite the bar, on the south side of the pass. Picnic anywhere; an especially good promontory (Lapa do Galho) is
about 12min from the road (2min before the first tunnel)

21 PICO REDONDO (large-scale pull-out map; photo page 104)

by car or taxi: 25–50min on foot   *by bus: 25–50min*
🚗 and 🚌 as Picnic 20 above; then use notes on page 105

22 LEVADA FALLS (large-scale pull-out map; photo page 100)

by car or taxi: 35min on foot   *by bus: 35min on foot*
🚗 and 🚌 as Picnic 20 above; then follow Walk 22 for 35 minutes

○25a PRAZERES (map page 113; photograph page 112)

by car or taxi: 5min on foot   *by bus: 30min on foot*
🚗Seacoast overlook in Prazeres: Turn south off the EN101 into the
village; past the church, keep forking right down to end of road
🚌107 to Prazeres: Follow Short walk on page 112 (30min)
This is a dramatic *coastal* setting

25b PRAZERES (map page 113; photograph page 113)

by car or taxi: 15–30min on foot   *by bus: 15–30min on foot*
🚗Prazeres, village square   🚌107 to Prazeres
Follow path of Walk 25 along the levada for *inland* setting

○26a CAMPO GRANDE (map page 120; photograph page 114)

by car or taxi: 5–45min on foot   *by bus and taxi: 5–45min*
🚗by the waterhouse on the EN208 (see page 115, line 7)
🚌 107 to Canhas *taxi rank* (see page 114) and *taxi to levada*
Picnic anywhere, perhaps by the caves (45min; Walk 26)

26b–d, 28 RABAÇAL (map and photographs pages 116–119)

by car or taxi: 0–25min on foot   *by bus and taxi: 0–25min*
🚗Rabaçal: Road is off the EN204 on the Paúl da Serra
🚌 107 to Canhas *taxi rank* (see page 114) and *taxi to Rabaçal*
There are four picnic choices from Rabaçal: 26b (by the houses),
26c (a sun-trap below the houses), 26d (far side of the tunnel, over-
looking Calheta's valley) and 28 (the Risco falls). **NB**: the road to
Rabaçal is very narrow; you may prefer to *walk* down to Rabaçal
Notes for Walks 26 and 28 describe these picnic settings

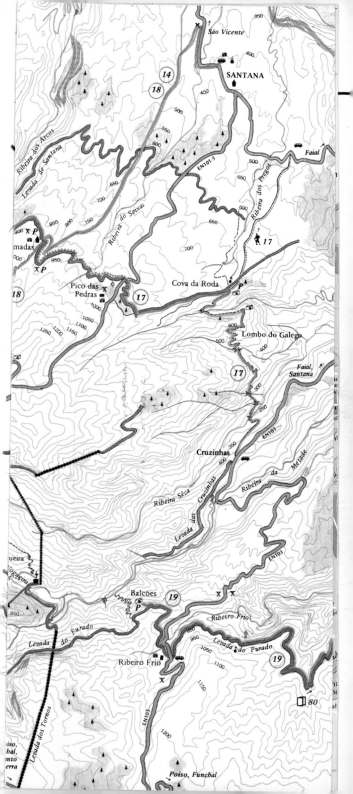

1 EASTERN MADEIRA'S GENTLE CHARMS

Palheiro Gardens · Camacha · Santo da Serra · Ponta de São Lourenço · Machico · Santa Cruz · Garajau · Funchal

A leisurely all-day tour on good, generally asphalted, roads. The Palheiro Gardens are open Monday to Friday (except holidays), but only in the morning (09.30—12.30); purchase tickets at the gate, or in advance at the Blandy agency in Funchal. Reckon on about 84km/52mi, about 4 hours' driving; take Exit A from Funchal (see map page 11)

On route: ✗ on the EN202 north of João Frino, Santa Cruz, Garajau; **P** (see pages 12—16) 7b, 8, 9, 10, 11, 12; Walks 7—13

Photo references: see below and pages 20, 21, 62, 65, 67, 68, 72—3, 74, 75, 76, 78, 84. In our picture book, *Madeira* (1987 edition), see pages 4, 18, 19, 56, 58, 59, 68, 80, 108—9, 120, 121

L eave Funchal by the EN102-1 (Rua Dr Manuel Pestana Junior — Exit A), and allow half an hour in morning traffic to reach the **Palheiro Gardens★** (5km) — on your right, just a few minutes after joining the EN102 (signposted south to São Gonçalo). Turn into the cobbled drive, shaded by magnificent planes and festooned with camelias and lilies. From the gate you can see only a fraction of the vast property. Gentle terraces sweep away below, yielding up ever-changing vistas of the formal and informal gardens, pools and fountains, avenues and parks surrounding the Count of Carvahal's original *quinta* and chapel.

When you leave the estate, turn right on the EN102, passing the road to Paradise Valley up left (**P**9) and then ✗ left and ♣ right. Climb up to **Camacha★** (10km ✗♣⊕WC), the centre of Madeira's willow-craft industry. The village square overlooks the magnificent Porto Novo valley (Walks 7 and 8). From Camacha keep climbing the EN102, past orchards and market gardens, to the wooded heights around the charming hamlet of **Eira de Fora**. There is a view down right over the Levada dos Tornos (Walks 7, 8), before you come to **Águas Mansas** (15km) and pass the junction of the EN206 south (**P**7b).

Oh, for a salad, so seldom seen on hotel tables! But these tender lettuces, grown at Assomada, are on sale at the market in Funchal

Then round a bend to marvel at the great willow-basin of the Boaventura river valley. At 19km pass the EN202 left to Poiso (🏔; *P*10), and at 21km fork right on the EN207 into **Santo da Serra** (22km 🏨✖🏛), a woodland village with gracious *quintas* and a golf course. Turn left just before the inn and follow a cobbled road beside the park: the steep, bucolic descent affords wonderful views over Machico's valley, before you reach the crossing of the EN101 at 24km. If you've been early birds, you may have time for a detour to Portela, 3.5km north (see notes on page 24).

Or follow with us: turn right, to meet the EN101-3 at 29km. Turn left here and climb the lush eastern flanks of Machico's valley (✖), soon meeting a tunnel (*P*12). Unless you have a reason to visit Caniçal, continue on the EN101-3 (✖) out to **São Lourenço Point**. Use the notes on pages 75–77 to explore this area, perhaps picnicking at Abra Bay (41km 📷*P*11). On your return from the point, take the road just west of the tunnel to **Pico do Facho** (50km 📷*P*12) to admire the views over Machico and its bay, nestling below the grey-green hills of Santo da Serra. Take care turning the car round in the tiny parking area before heading on into **Machico** (56km 🏨✖🏛⊕🛉🛉). Much island history attaches to Machico, Madeira's first settlement. Of particular interest are the Manueline church and the Chapel of Miracles. The latter, on the east side of the river, was founded in 1420 on the site of Zarco's first landfall; destroyed by a great flood in 1803, the chapel was rebuilt later in the 19th century.

The enchanting gardens at Palheiro Ferreiro are only open in the morning. After your visit, why not explore a bit along the levada paths described in Walk 7?

Just outside Machico, don't miss a side road up right to a viewpoint (📷). from where you will have a new perspective on the flawless setting of emerald-green Machico Bay, Pico do Facho, and the sun-baked arm of São Lourenço. Returning to the EN101, now pass the giant beehives of the island's largest holiday resort, **Matur** (🏨✕), before coming into delightful **Santa Cruz** (63km ⚓✕✕🏛), where you may visit the *til*-shaded village square with its fine bright-white Manueline buildings, among them the fifteenth-century Church of São Salvador and the town hall.

Pass again the EN206 branching right to Gaula (*P*7b) and soon cross the great cleft of the Porto Novo Valley east of Assomada (*P*8). Just past the EN205 leading up right to Camacha, we turn left down to **Caniço** (74km 🏨✕🏛⊕), a market-garden and tourist centre. Negotiate the one-way circuit, then head right, down a steep cobbled road, to **Garajau Point** (76km † 📷 ✕). From this sunny promontory, spiked with pricky-pear cactus and Pride of Madeira, you have a splendid panorama of the Desertas Islands and São Lourenço Point to the east and the comings and goings of ships around the Bay of Funchal just west. The statue here, to Christ the King, is a miniature of the famous one in Rio de Janeiro; it is best appreciated from the sea.

On leaving Garajau, don't return to Caniço but head up northwest, to regain the EN101 by **Cancela** (78km ✕🏛). Be sure not to take the new road here, but stay on the old EN101-11, the narrow road hugging the coast. Look out, 2km past Cancela, for a fine promontory on the left (📷) called 'The Pinnacle', from where the views over Funchal are superb. Then pass **São Gonçalo** (81km ✕🏛); from here it's just 3km to central Funchal. You will pass another bougainvilla-fringed overlook (📷) closer to the city centre.

2 THE CORRAL AND THE CAPE

Pico dos Barcelos · Eira do Serrado · Curral das Freiras · Câmara de Lobos · Cabo Girão · Funchal

This tour is suitable for morning or afternoon, but we would suggest taking almost a day. Road conditions will slow you down. The EN215 and EN101 between Funchal and Cabo Girão are heavily congested. The road to Curral das Freiras is not for the faint-hearted: mostly cobbled, it flaunts many hairpin bends and sheer drops past the Eira do Serrado. Reckon on 71km/44mi, about 4 hours' driving; take Exit B from Funchal (map page 10)

On route: ✗ at the Cabo Girão *miradouro; P* (see pages 12—16) 1, 4; Walks 1—4

Photo references: see pages 22, 43, 49, 53. In our picture book, *Madeira* (1987 edition), see pages 16, 17, 30, 31, 54, 55, 62, 63, 95, 106

L eaving Funchal by the EN215 (Rua do Dr Pita — Exit B), approach the church of São Martinho — an island landmark — on a hill. Turn right just before the church, climbing the EN105 to **Pico dos Barcelos★** (6km ☎WC✗). From this aloe-collared *miradouro* the views of the Funchal setting and the eastern arm of the island are very fine. About 1.5km further north on the EN105, join the EN107 and climb through forests of eucalyptus and pine splintered by golden sun-shafts. A good viewpoint (☎) over the Socorridos ravine is passed on the left before reaching the right-hand fork to the **Eira do Serrado★** (16km ☎WC; 15min return on foot for truly stupendous views over Curral — 400m/1300ft below). Beyond the Eira the road becomes increasingly vertiginous as it circles down into **Curral das Freiras** (The Nuns' Corral, 20km WC), ringed round by awesome heights. The village is a focal point for some of the island's most challenging walks.

Return to São Martinho, taking a right turn before the church and following the (unnumbered) secondary road down to the EN215 (38km). Turn right (*P*1) and cross the mighty Socorridos, to see the majestic cliff of Cabo Girão. At the crossroad (✗♨) into **Câmara de Lobos★**, notice the terrace on the left. It was from here that Sir Winston Churchill painted the curving white arc of the village against the backdrop of the red cape. The area between the church (⚓ founded by Zarco 1424) and the sea has been closed to

Car tour 1: lovely Abra Bay, setting for Picnic 11

traffic by our friend Sidonio, who runs the delightful Coral Restaurant (✘) with its breath-taking view. Stop in for a coffee, then drive on for 1km to find a signpost to a good viewpoint up right (📷) at **Pico da Torre**. Now follow the winding EN101 as far as the left-hand turn to **Cabo Girão★** (51km 📷✘✘WC). Here, safe behind iron railings, marvel at the toy ships at sea 580m/1900ft below — and at the tenacity of the sure-footed Madeiran farmers working their tiny terraces. Return east on the EN101 to a fork up left to **Estreito** (56km ✘), where the island's best grapes are grown. From here it's under 15km back to Funchal. A visit to Jardim da Serra (**P**4; see page 13) will add 14km (1½h) to your tour.

The heights above Curral, seen from the aloe-fringed Eira do Serrado

3 MOUNTAINS AND MORE MOUNTAINS!

Terreiro da Luta · Poiso · Arieiro · Portela · Porto da Cruz · Faial · Santana · Achada do Teixeira · Ribeiro Frio · Funchal

Start out early in the morning and aim to reach Arieiro no later than 09.30; clouds often descend at about 10.00, obscuring the wonderful views from the peaks. Although this tour is a long one, the roads are generally asphalted and quite good. Reckon on 138km/86mi, about 6 hours' driving; take Exit A from Funchal (see map page 11)

On route: X at Poiso, EN202 north of João Frino, EN103 around Ribeiro Frio, Pico das Pedras, EN101-5, path from Achada do Teixeira to Pico Ruivo, Queimadas Park; *P* (see pages 12—16) 9, 10, 14, 15, 17, 18, 19a, 19b; Walks 9, 10, 14—19

Photo references: see pages 20, 24, 29, 65, 68, 86, 88, 97, 98. In our picture book, *Madeira* (1987 edition), see pages 2—3, 6—7, 22, 26, 27, 32—33, 34—35, 46, 47, 52, 66, 67, 72, 73, 92—93, 94, 96—97, 110—111, 112—113, 114—115, 130—131, 132—133, 139

It is usual to include the mountainous northeast of the island in what is often called a 'Santana Tour', covering central Madeira (our Tour 4). We find this very hectic and urge you to devote an entire day to visiting the great rugged peaks and the gentle moorland roads radiating from Poiso Pass. This tour fits in nicely with No 5, providing a leisurely two-day introduction to many of Madeira's best landscapes.

The direct route to Pico do Arieiro from Funchal is via Exit C (Rua 31 de Janeiro — EN103), passing Monte. But we suggest you try another way: take Exit A and use the notes on page 18 as far as the Palheiro Gardens (5km). In a minute more, you will encounter the EN201 joining from the left. Turn up northwest here and follow this gentle, dusty-red pine- and eucalyptus-shaded road to **Terreiro da Luta★** (14km † ⌖ WC). Here a statue to Our Lady of Peace commemorates the sufferings of the people of Funchal during World War I. Round the base of the statue there is a rosary made from the anchor chains of ships torpedoed in Funchal harbour. In the early 1900s a luxurious funicular railway climbed up here via Monte. The views over the city's setting are superb, but soon you must *press on!* Join the EN103 ahead and turn right. The smooth asphalt road lined with hydrangeas and lilies snakes its way up to a barren plateau and finally **Poiso Pass** (1400m/4600ft; 20km XX). Here turn left on the highland road (EN202) to Arieiro. Sheep dart about in the morning mists, munching gorse and bilberry — *take care!*

Make straight for the end of the road, **Pico do Arieiro★** (1818m/5963ft; 27km ⌖ WC ⌂ X X P18, described page 96). On your return to Poiso, be sure to make a stop at another viewpoint a few minutes below Arieiro on the left (⌖): it's just 15min return on foot to the **Miradouro do Juncal**, from where you have glorious views of the sweep of the Metade

Descending into Porto da Cruz from the west: The eastern headlands – setting for Walk 13 – stretch to the distant arm of São Lourenço

Valley down to Faial and the Penha de Águia (Eagle Rock). Later in the day, you will have another 'eagle's eye' view of the Metade, from Balcões. Pass the meteorological station and come again to Poiso (34km). From here go straight ahead on the EN202 opposite — a moorland road — one of the loveliest on Madeira (**x**; *P*10).

When you meet the EN102 (42km), turn left, passing the EN207 into Santo da Serra (**&**) and continuing up (*P*19b) under deep shade to **Portela** (49km **⊡x**). Here you enjoy a superb outlook to the north coast and down over Machico's green valley. From Portela take the EN101 down into bright **Porto da Cruz** (55km **x&**). A good viewpoint (**⊡**) over the village is met on leaving, as you climb up west to skirt round the towering mass of Eagle Rock. Soon Faial comes into view, and there is a splendid panorama from the bridge over the Metade River (**⊡**). Pass the EN103 on your left (60km **x**), enter **Faial** and then make for Santana, ignoring for the moment two viewpoints over Faial. The sun is now too high for this landscape to be seen at its best.

With good planning you will reach the Santana area near lunchtime. Before entering the village centre, turn left (after 68km) on the EN101-5 (2 **⊡** and **x**) for **Pico das Pedras** (△**x** with fireplaces) and **Achada do Teixeira** (79km **⊡x**). If you have time for a *leisurely* picnic, you can choose Queimadas Park (*P*14), Homem em Pé or Pico Ruivo (*P*15), or Cova da Roda (*P*17). See picnicking notes on page 15. To picnic at either Queimadas or Cova da Roda, park by the levada below Pico das Pedras forestry house. (Note that although the EN101-5 is signposted to Queimadas, you can only *walk* to Queimadas Park from here.) To picnic at Homem em Pé or on the Ruivo path, park at Achada do Teixeira, where the EN101-5 ends.

On your return from Achada do Teixeira, continue on the EN101 to **Santana★** (90km ♦×♣). Madeira's 'most picturesque village' surpasses its reputation: it's an enchantment of delightful thatched cottages, glorious flowers, patchwork-quilt gardens, rolling hills and orchards, set against a background of spectacular mountain scenery. Just over 1km west of the Achada do Teixeira road, an old cobbled road leads steeply uphill to Queimadas Park. Once you're on this narrow, poorly-paved road, there's no turning back beyond the last houses! It's usually easier to walk to Queimadas from Pico das Pedras, unless you're lucky enough to come when the road is newly tarred!

It's now afternoon. Return to Faial. You are just in time to get the best views from the two *miradouros* (☜) west of the village. Clouds scud across the sky, creating fascinating mosaics of light and shade on this dramatic landscape. Eagle Rock is seen from base to summit, standing guard over church and village, at the confluence of three great river valleys: the Metade, the Sêca and the São Roque. This superb panorama is likely to be one of your most lasting impressions of Madeira. As you climb out of Faial, turn right on the EN103 (99km ×). Look left to see São Roque (photo page 86) atop its *lombo* — the spine separating two parallel ravines — as you follow the road up the spectacularly-terraced Metade Valley as far as the tiny hamlet of **Cruzinhas** (104km). A great bend now takes the road past fruit trees and forests of cedar, cypress, pine and eucalyptus, to the gentle environs of Ribeiro Frio. There are several well-placed picnic sites (✗) along the way, before you come to a viewpoint (☜) left over the valley. Soon reach the sweet coolness of **Ribeiro Frio★** (109km WC ✗ and ☜: 45min return on foot). Take a break here to visit the trout hatcheries, the small botanical gardens and **Balcões** — the 'balconies' (*P* 19a). The path (signposted) to this viewpoint is just north of the trout farm. Follow its flower-lined meanderings beside the dry levada; in twenty minutes you'll pass through a cut in the towering, moss-covered basalt and find yourself high in the Metade Valley. Soon come to a fork, where an old levada goes left; turn right and you're at Balcões in a minute. It's a view to contrast with that from the Juncal outlook earlier today. Eagle Rock is seen again, presiding over the north coast villages of Porto da Cruz and Faial. But from Balcões the jagged central peaks dominate the scene: Arieiro, Ruivo and the Torres. The Metade takes its source on these heights,

Serra de Água's golden valley — above: seen from Lapa do Galho (Picnic 20); below: the southern reaches, near Ribeira Brava

and its waters feed the power station 250m/820ft below you, from where they flow on in the Tornos levada to irrigate the fields between Funchal and Santa Cruz.

There are more picnic tables as you climb round and round out of Ribeiro Frio, through a conifer forest, to meet again the moorlands of Poiso (115km ✗✗). There's one more road from Poiso which you have still to discover: the EN203, a forestry road, signposted left to Camacha half a kilometre south of the pass. This delightful route offers picnicking and walking possibilities all the way down, as you overlook the church of Gaula and the Desertas. When you lose the moorland to gorse, ferns and pine, you'll soon cross the Levada da Serra at Paradise Valley (✗P9). Half a kilometre further on, meet the EN102 (122km ✗). Turn *left*, to find the EN205 (🛐) south to Caniço about 1.5km east. This cobbled road affords a picture of rural Madeira (see page 19) that will delight you. Turn right on the EN101 to return to Funchal (138km). If you have time, and have not yet seen Garajau Point, use the notes on page 20 to make this detour, which will add under 2km to the tour.

4 MADEIRA NORTH AND SOUTH

Ribeira Brava · Encumeada · São Vicente · Boaventura ·
Santana · Faial · Ribeiro Frio · Poiso · Monte · Funchal

*If you've already done Tour 3, you can take this one in your stride,
even though you will encounter some heavy traffic in the south and
winding cobbled roads in the north. But if you plan any detours —
to the mountains or Porto Moniz (via São Vicente, see page 30) —
you're in for a hectic and tiring day. Be warned also: you are very
likely to meet tour buses hurtling along the narrow north coast
road; you may even be forced to back up quite some distance to let
them pass! Plan on covering 129km/80mi, about 6—7 hours' driving;
take Exit D from Funchal (map page 10)*

On route: ✕ at Campanário, Vinháticos, Encumeada, Chão dos
Louros, Queimadas Park, EN101-5, Pico das Pedras, path from
Achada to Pico Ruivo, EN103 around Ribeiro Frio; ***P*** (see pages 12–
16) 6a, 6b, 7a, 14, 15, 17, 18, 19a, 20, 21, 22; Walks 5, 6, 14–24

Photo references: See pages 26, 28, 29, 61, 62, 64, 86, 88, 97, 98,
100, 104. In our picture book, *Madeira* (1987 edition), see pages
6–7, 16–17, 22, 26–27, 28–29, 34–35, 46–47, 50–51, 52, 57,
66–67, 70, 73, 79, 81, 92–93, 96–97, 104, 105, 107, 110–111,
112–113, 114–115, 122–123, 124–125, 126, 130–131, 132–133,
138, 139, 140

I f you've only one day in which to tour Madeira, this is the
circuit to make, but start out *very* early, so that you can
include an excursion to one of the peaks. Leave Funchal by
the EN215 (Estrada Monumental — Exit D). Pass **Câmara
de Lobos** and **Cabo Girão** (EN101; see page 21) and then
Quinta Grande and **Campanário** (✕***P***6a, 6b), before circling
steeply down into cheerful **Ribeira Brava** (31km ▲▲✕⊕♨ and
⚓ founded in the 1500s). Take a break here for coffee in
the plane-shaded esplanade, before leaving the village on the
EN104 north, along a narrow canyon graced with poplars.
Pass **Serra de Água** and two ✕ before reaching the beautifully-
situated Pousada dos Vinháticos (41km ▣▲✕✕). Then continue to **Encumeada** (1004m/3293ft; 44km ▣ ✕ *P* 20–22).
   From this pass there are wonderful views over the north
and south coasts. While you are here, *do* take the oppor-
tunity to see the great Levada do Norte; it's just a minute's
walk from the parking area — the steps are opposite the bar
on the south side of the pass (notes page 101). Then descend
into São Vicente's welcoming valley, past a fine laurel grove,
Chão dos Louros (46km WC ✕ with fireplaces). Soon you'll
have good views over **Rosário's** church and stream: in high
summer Rosário's hay-ricks weave ribbons of gold into the
tapestry of this emerald landscape. Pass the village and soon
come to a new road climbing over 1400m/4595ft to the
Paúl da Serra (via Ginjas, on your left). On your right, on
the eastern hillside, there is a graceful clocktower — Nossa
Senhora da Fâtima — a landmark on several island walks.

Come into **São Vicente** (55km ✗♨️♨️ with a painting of the village on its ceiling and ♨️ built into a hollowed-out rock south of the bridge). Part of the village has been lovingly restored by the tourism department. Turn right on the coastal EN101 (56km ✗). Immediately your attention will be drawn to the chequered pattern made by the heath tree hedges protecting the terraces from the fierce northerly winds. Most of the fields are planted with vines, but this is for table wine; the vines which yield the grapes for the fine Madeira wines are generally found in the south, around Estreito. The cobbled road becomes ever narrower, passing in shadow below a menacing cliff, before skirting above the lava-fertile promontory of **Ponta Delgada** (62km ✗♨️) and soaring up to a viewpoint (📷) over the village setting and headlands to the east. Almost immediately the road turns inland, leaving the awesome coast for the green-gold gentleness of the great **Boaventura** valley. Just past the village (65km), there is a good *miradouro* (📷) on the left. At the head of the valley you will see roadworks. A road will be

The Pousada dos Vinháticos, an idyllic retreat. This countryside inn is ideally situated for walkers

The mountainous interior, seen from Balcões (Picnic 19a)

built from here to Curral das Freiras — a continuation of the EN107 (see map).

The bucolic pleasures of this valley are a foretaste of the whole unforgettable landscape between Boaventura and Santana. Pass above **Arco de São Jorge** (72km), decked out with vines and hedgerows and rainbows of flowers. The hillsides are cultivated almost down to the sea, along the sweeping curve (*arco*) of the bay. Climb past mossy cliffs and dark pines brightened by banks of agapanthus, to reach another outlook by a sea-cliff (☞✗). From here there are excellent views over Arco and back to Ponta Delgada, where the church and a swimming pool are down by the seashore. Adjacent to this viewpoint is 'Cabanas' (⚑✗). The road surface improves for the descent to **São Jorge** (82km ⚲), which boasts the richest baroque church outside Funchal. Soon hairpin bends offer enticing views of **Santana★**, where orchards and market gardens roll down to the sea.

The route now travels via the EN101 and EN103 from Santana to Poiso (notes pages 25 and 26). It's about two hours from Santana to Funchal. If you've not done the 'Mountains' tour, and you have the time, we'd suggest driving to Pico das Pedras and walking to Queimadas or Cova da Roda. Or press on to Ribeiro Frio and Balcões, and from Poiso, make a 14km (return) trip to Pico do Arieiro★ (*P*18).

Past **Poiso** (115km *excluding detours*), continue south on the EN103 to **Monte★** (123km ✗⚲⚲). Walk above the delightful gardens to the Church of Our Lady of the Mount, where you may see the tiny poignant statue to Madeira's patron saint. From the bottom of the church steps (departure point for the famous toboggan rides), follow the agapanthus-banked lane left around to **Babosas** (☞*P*7a; ten minutes return on foot: see notes page 69). Here a baroque chapel looks out over the impressive bowl of Curral dos Romeiros (photo page 64). It's just 5km back to Funchal.

5 PORTO MONIZ AND PAÚL DA SERRA

Ribeira Brava · São Vicente · Seixal · Porto Moniz · Ribeira
da Janela Valley · Paúl da Serra · Canhas · Funchal

*This is the easiest tour to the west of the island. The EN204 across
the Paúl da Serra not only cuts an hour's driving off the south coast
route, but affords motorists superb views over a landscape pre-
viously accessible only to walkers. Expect hectic driving on the
EN215 and EN101. You will also have to go slowly on the narrow
corniche road between São Vicente and Porto Moniz — where you
are likely to encounter tour coaches, especially in the afternoon. If
you plan to do Tours 4 and 6, you might try this one in reverse, to
see the same landscapes at a different time of day. Plan on 158km/
98mi, 7–8 hours' driving; take Exit D from Funchal (map page 10)*

On route: ✗ at Campanário, Vinháticos, Encumeada, Chão dos
Louros, Fonte do Bispo, Rabaçal, EN208; ***P*** (see pages 12—16) 6a,
6b, 20, 21, 22, 26a—d, 28; Walks 5, 6, 20—24, 26—28

Photo references: see pages 26, 28, 31, 61, 62, 100, 104, 114—115,
116, 117, 118, 119. In our picture book, *Madeira* (1987 edition),
see pages 10, 14—15, 16—17, 23, 28—29, 50—51, 57, 70, 81, 86,
90, 98—99, 104, 105, 107, 116—117, 119, 122—123, 124—125

This tour combines especially well with the 'Mountains'
circuit, to provide a two-day programme covering *almost*
all of Madeira's best landscapes, without any duplication of
routes. Until recently, the usual approach to Porto Moniz
was via the southwest coastal road, returning by Encumeada
— a very long drive, especially for those staying at Machico
or Matur. What's more, very few visitors saw the magnificent
Paúl da Serra, and only walkers could appreciate the valley
of the Ribeira da Janela. The southwest coastal road is well
worth pursuing (see our Tour 6); but if you have only one
day to see the west, then *this* is the tour to make.

Leave Funchal by the EN215 (Estrada Monumental —
Exit D). Use notes on page 27 to **São Vicente** (55km). North
of the village, turn left on the justly-famed corniche road to
Porto Moniz: for fifteen kilometres it soars up cliffs and
swoops down again to the sea, racing in single-minded deter-
mination through tunnels and waterfalls. *Drive slowly and
carefully; sound your horn at blind corners; lights on in the
tunnels.* (The edge of the road is generally built up with
solid concrete; motorists should not find it vertiginous.)

There are three viewpoints (🕿) on the route. The first is
at a tunnel 2km east of **Seixal** (63km ✗⊕), a village perched
high on a promontory, where a graceful church looks out
over terrifyingly steep vineyards. It is said that here the
feathery heath tree hedges not only protect the crops from
the wind, but the farmers from falling into the sea! The next
viewpoint is at another tunnel, just after you pass *through*
waterfalls! Here you look out east past Seixal, as far as São
Jorge; in the foreground, the falls cascade over towering

30

cliffs where Pride of Madeira clings tenaciously. West lies **Ribeira da Janela**: village and river take their name from the 'window' (*janela*) in the lava rock off the shore. Just past the mouth of the great river is the final outlook over this dramatic coastal landscape; then round a bend (⚓) and you are in **Porto Moniz★** (72km ⛺△✕⚓). Here reefs in the coastal lava rocks create a maze of glassy sea-water pools where you may swim or picnic — if you don't mind the cool breezes. Climbing out of the village on the steep hairpin bends of the EN101, you'll find two bird's-eye viewpoints (📷) over the village setting, before passing **Santa** and then meeting the EN204 southeast (after 78km).

Turn left and follow the EN204 for eighteen kilometres along the course of Madeira's greatest valley. The far-off views over north and south coasts are splendid. But even more impressive is the size and magnificence of the Janela ravine. Virgin forests of heath and laurel cloak the mountainsides like coats of green sable. You'll pass several good lookouts (📷) on the road: one of the finest is at the old ruined 'Casa do Elias' at Quebradas (83km). From here you have the best view imaginable over the village of Ribeira da Janela on its conical, grove-hatted hilltop. Soon come to another *miradouro* near **Fonte do Bispo** (from where a new road — the EN210 — will be built down to sunny Prazeres; 88km 📷✕). If you have brought binoculars, looking southeast you can see the red-roofed Rabaçal houses at the head of the valley and even the Risco waterfall. Across the valley, on a hill, find a curiously bare area, studded with trees. This is the idyllic Fanal, where some of the island's indigenous great laurels are still to be found. Beyond the Fanal, the mighty peaks in the east rise above cloud necklaces. In the west, a lighthouse is glimpsed at Ponta do Pargo.

At 96km, past the EN211 south to Calheta, you reach the head of the valley, by a reservoir. Here you are just

You'll glimpse the Fanal — a parkland of ancient trees — from the EN204. The area is now under government protection (Tours 5, 6)

above Rabaçal, the island beauty spot much beloved by
Madeirans. A detour down the *very narrow* road adds 4km
to the tour: notes about the area, a map, and photographs,
are found on pages 114—119 (*P* 26b—d, *P* 28).

Past the Rabaçal road, you approach the moorland vistas
of the Paúl da Serra, so very different from the Janela valley
— and any other Madeiran landscape! Even in rainy weather
the Paúl has a strange beauty: the moors take on a golden
hue, the bracken throws up wine-red flames, and sea birds
swirl over the marshes. On sunny days, the air is always
bright as diamonds.

You'll reach the EN208 south (signposted to Canhas and
Funchal) at 100km. Turn down right, leaving the Paúl and
Campo Grande's highlands (†*P* 26a) for dark forests and
market gardens (✕✕), before meeting the EN101 at 113km.
Turn left (♞) for the journey from Canhas to Funchal,
described — in reverse — on the facing page.

6 THE SUNNY SOUTHWEST COAST

Ribeira Brava · Canhas · Arco da Calheta · Prazeres · Ponta do Pargo · Ribeira da Janela Valley · Paúl da Serra · Funchal

Although roads are being asphalted, much of the way between Ponta do Sol and the EN204 may still be cobbled, making for tiring driving. The tour is described from the (higher) vantage point of the EN101. If you find endless sorties into and out of valleys irksome, you can travel on direct coastal roads from Ribeira Brava to Calheta. The route described covers about 175km/109mi; 8–9 hours' driving; however, diversions to the coast at Prazeres, Raposeira or Fajã da Ovelha are recommended. Take exit D from Funchal (map page 10)

On route: X at Campanário, Ponta do Sol, Prazeres, Fonte do Bispo, Rabaçal, EN208; *P* (see pages 12–16) 6a, 6b, 25a, 25b, 26a–d, 28; Walks 5, 6, 25–28

Photo references: see opposite and pages 31, 61, 62, 112–113, 114–115, 116, 117, 118, 119. In our picture book, *Madeira* (1987 edition), see pages 8–9, 16–17, 24–25, 28–29, 36, 38–39, 42, 46, 86, 90, 98–99, 116–117, 119

The notes on page 27 will take you to Ribeira Brava (31km). Notice the pleasant village setting as you climb out along the EN101. Pass above **Tábua** and below **Lombada da Ponta do Sol** (♠), where sugar cane plantations flourished in the 1500s. The road (X) then continues above **Ponta do Sol** (38km ♠ and ♠ founded in the 15th century). Go on (♠) through pretty **Canhas** (41km ♠). Just beyond the church, on the right, notice the first of fourteen statues representing the Stations of the Cross; after the last, on a straight stretch of road (♠), there is a monument to St Theresa (†). Soon (43km) pass the EN208 leading up right to the Paúl da Serra.

Soon come to two truly astounding outlooks straight down over the sparkling houses and banana trees of Madalena do Mar 375m/1250ft below (☞ and ☞X).

Interesting churches (♠), where much is preserved from the days of their founding, are to be found at the three Calhetas. The first is the Manueline **Loreto** chapel at **Arco da Calheta**, on the left, just past a road up right to a viewpoint (☞) at Pico do Arco. The next is the 15th century mother church in **Calheta** (♠⊕), 3km south of the EN101 (X). The third is at **Estreito da Calheta**: the 16th century Reis Magos chapel.

Climb under mimosa to **Prazeres** (X*P*25a, 25b) and **Raposeira**, before passing the turning left to Fajã da Ovelha. At **Ponta do Pargo** (79km) the second, tarred road left leads to the lighthouse (81km ☞). It's about 16km to the EN204 east; the route from there to Canhas is described on page 31.

Left: The coastal EN101 is lush with vegetation. Levadas great and small criss-cross the land. Their waters rise in the springs of the Paúl da Serra. The grey, sun-dappled flanks of the moorland paint a sombre backdrop for the golden fields in the south (Tour 6)

✵ Walking

In this third edition, we've added several walks, but the major change in the walking section is the redrawn *maps reproduced in full colour*. We hope that the addition of contour lines, woodlands, etc, will be helpful and will give you a better feeling for the terrain.

By following the walks in this book, you can *cross the island on foot*. We've shown where walks link up, both on the walking maps and the touring map. Of course, you can also make up your own walk combinations, but please: never try to get from one walk to another on uncharted terrain! This is far too dangerous on Madeira. Only link up walks by following our notes or by using roads or tracks!

Beginners: There are many suitable walks for you. Start with those described as easy under 'Grade', and be sure to check all the short and alternative walks — some are easy versions of the long walks for experts.

Experienced walkers: If you are accustomed to rough terrain and have a head for heights, you should be able to take all the walks in this book (except those labelled Ⓖ) in your stride. Provided, of course, that storm damage has not made the way unsafe, and *provided that you follow the route as we describe it*. If you have not reached one of our landmarks after a reasonable time, you must go back to the last 'sure' point and start again.

Experts: You should not need a guide for any of the 28 walks described, provided that you are used to very sheer unprotected drops. We've also alerted you to other walks you might wish to tackle with a guide: these are indicated in the text, in parentheses, *in italic type*. None of these paths should be attempted outside high summer!

Guides, waymarking, maps

Several walks (or sections of walks) are labelled Ⓖ. We believe that everyone excepting **expert** walkers should go with a guide along these paths. In some cases, this is because you could lose your way in heavy mists; more often it is because a path is especially vertiginous or hazardous under certain conditions. For example, you cannot 'get lost' on the north coast path between Boca do Risco and Porto da Cruz, but only someone who knows that path well will know if it is too muddy or scree-covered to continue the

34

walk. People unaccustomed to walking on Madeira — where conditions change very rapidly — might be tempted to go on under extremely hazardous conditions. The same applies to levadas: when the channel is too dangerous to pass, the beginner may not realise that a path must be found to skirt around the narrow lip of the levada channel.

Guides may sometimes be found in mountain villages; a few taxi drivers also act as guides. However, we recommend that you book an **approved guide** at the Tourist Office.

Do *not* rely on **waymarking**. There is very little signposting on the island at present. In future years, some of the more popular walks may be waymarked.

For all the routes described in this book, the maps we've drawn are the most useful you will find. They are based on our own tape-recorded walking notes and large-scale engineering maps not generally available. A two-sheet map of the island (1:50,000; 1915, revised 1970) is available in Funchal from Agência João Silvério Pires, 20 Avenida Zarco. It is very useful regarding contours and heights, but bear in mind that many of the paths indicated on it are no longer viable!

Walkers' checklist
The following pointers cannot be stressed too often:
- At any time a walk may become unsafe due to storm damage. If the route is not as we describe it and your way ahead is not secure, do not attempt to go on.
- Walks labelled Ⓖ are generally unsuitable for winter walking, and all walks in the north may be very wet in winter.
- Never walk alone — four is the best walking group.
- Do not overestimate your energies: your speed will be determined by the slowest walker in the group.
- Bus connections at the end of a walk are vital.
- Proper shoes or boots are a necessity.
- Mists can fall suddenly anywhere, especially on the Paúl da Serra and in the mountains.
- Warm clothing is needed in the mountains.
- Compass, whistle, torch weigh little, but might save your life.
- Extra rations must be taken on long walks.
- Always wear a sunhat after 10 am.
- A stout stick is a help on steep terrain and to discourage the rare unfriendly dog.
- Do not panic in an emergency.
- Read and re-read the important note on page 2 and the country code on page 40, as well as guidelines on grade and equipment for each walk you plan to make.

Where to stay

If you are going to Madeira purely for a walking holiday, we'd suggest that you spend one week in Funchal (to enjoy the walks in the south- and northeast of the island) and a week at the beautifully-situated Pousada dos Vinháticos (from where you can quite easily get to the walks in the centre and west of Madeira).

If you have only a week, or if walking is not your top priority, then it's best to stay in Funchal. The bus network radiates from the capital, affording all the best connections. All our walks are written up based on Funchal. However, since many people stay in the Caniço—Matur—Machico axis, we've included a great many walks in the southeast.

Rest house* accommodation is booked at the Tourist Office or the President's House. Bring your own provisions; cooking facilities and bedding are provided. **See STOP PRESS for more details.**

*The **Ruivo** rest house is run by the *Tourist Office for visitors*; others are run by the *government for its staff*, and are often fully booked

Weather

The summer months — May to September — afford the best walking on Madeira: not only is the weather fine, but the island enjoys moderate temperatures. The autumnal rains begin late in September and carry on into December: these often take the form of violent, intermittent showers. March and April also bring showery, windy days. In winter, the weather is more settled, but wetter. While this thumbnail sketch of Madeira's seasons holds true generally, rainfall varies greatly from year to year all round the island — the only constant being that rainfall in the north is always at least twice that in the south!

Safe walking demands accurate reading of the weather signs coupled with common sense. Outside summer months, and especially between November and March, many walks, especially in the north and west, become treacherous. Even on the most glorious winter's day, levada paths will be full to overflowing and some mountain trails like waterfalls, due to previous heavy rainfall. For this reason, **we recommend that you do not undertake any walk labelled Ⓖ in winter,** no matter how fine the day. And bear in mind that other walks in the north and west — such as the levada walks at Queimadas and Campo Grande, or the trail to Pináculo — might be exceedingly wet and potentially hazardous.

We've done *all* our walks outside summer months, by applying common sense to the following weather signs.

Apart from the **seasons**, Madeira's weather is determined by **wind direction**. From May to September the mild north-east trade winds prevail, affording fine and settled weather, with a steady barometer. Even outside summer months, the weather will still be at its best when the wind is from a northerly or easterly direction. If it swings round to due west or to the southwest, a fluctuating barometer and unsettled weather follow.

Since the central mountain chain catches up the clouds carried by these winds buffeting the island, you can read the wind signs to find the best 'microweather' for your walks!

■ **Strong winds** from any direction except east, bring rain, if not storms. Walking will not be good anywhere on the island if the barometer falls below 29.90″ (1012.58mbar). If it is steady at this reading or above, walks may be attempted in that part of the island protected from the wind and rain (thus, when a strong northeasterly wind carries rain to the Ribeiro Frio area, we would try a walk in the southwest).

■ **Strong wind from the east or south of east** ('leste'): this hot, dry wind from Africa guarantees good walking everywhere, with crystal clear views on the heights. But if the wind slips round to south, then west of south, storms will follow.

■ **Mild winds from any direction except south or south-west** afford good walking all round the island.

■ **Mild winds from south or southwest** generally carry rain within 24 hours, but with the barometer steady at 29.90″ (1012.58mbar), you may get in a day's walking in the east.

■ As a rule of thumb, the **Desertas Islands** can serve as a 'ready-reckoner' for weather signs:

— If the Desertas are clearly visible (wind from W of N), the south-east, northeast and east are clear — at least in the valleys. The west is cloudy.
— If the Desertas are hardly visible (wind from the E, SE): the south may be cloudy, but walking is generally good everywhere.
— If the Desertas are cloudy (wind from NE): the west, southwest, and northwest are clear; eastern areas may be cloudy.
— If the Desertas seem very close and there is a white line on the horizon (wind from S, SW), rain is coming within 24 hours.

■ **Meteorological charts** are available after 12.30h, *on request*, at the Tourist Office. For these other reports and forecasts, you will need the help of a Portuguese speaker:

— Radio Madeira forecasts the next day's weather at 21.00h
— Local newspapers (available after 07.00h) give daily forecasts
— Weather bureau (Protecção Civil) may be telephoned: 6.46.04

■ All round the island, the general pattern is a clear morning, with clouds gathering by mid-day, and the sky clearing again by mid-afternoon. **Early starts are recommended!**

What to take

If you are already on Madeira and haven't walking boots or a torch or rucksack, you can still make many of our walks. But don't attempt the more difficult ones without proper equipment. For each walk in this book, we tell you the *minimum* equipment necessary. Where we require walking boots, there is, unfortunately, no substitute: you will need to rely on the grip and ankle support they provide, as well as their waterproof qualities. All other walks should be made with stout shoes, preferably with thick rubber or 'Vibram'-type soles, to grip on wet, mossy surfaces. Do *not* venture on walks requiring a torch unless you have one — some levada tunnels are exceedingly long and you *must* be able to see both the roof (for possible projections) and the path, because the water in the channel may be very deep, cold, and fast-moving.

If, like us, you become addicted to walking on Madeira, you may find the following checklist useful:

walking boots (which *must* be broken in and comfortable)
waterproof rain gear (outside summer months)
plastic bottle and water purifying tablets
torch (preferably throwing a *wide* beam)
long sleeved shirt for sun protection
long trousers, tight at the ankles
bandages and band-aids
small rucksack
whistle
compass
plastic plates, cups, etc
knives and openers
anorak (zip opening)
2 light cardigans
map (see page 35)
bus timetable
sunhat
plastic rain hat
extra pair of socks
spare bootlaces
plastic groundsheet

Please bear in mind that we've not made *every* walk in this book under *all* weather conditions: we may not realise just how hot — or wet — some walks can be! Outside the summer months, boots are always more useful than shoes — especially on overflowing levadas. In hot weather, *always* carry a long-sleeved shirt as well as your sun hat, and take your lunch in a shady spot. We rely on your good judgement to modify our equipment lists according to the season.

Portuguese for walkers

In Funchal you hardly need know any Portuguese at all, but once you venture off the beaten track you may want to ask directions and *no one* can speak English. We have found an almost foolproof way to ask *and understand* directions in Portuguese. First, memorise the key questions and all their possible answers below; then always phrase your questions so that you will get a yes (*sim*) or no (*não*) answer.

The key questions (English/Portuguese/approximate pronunciation)

'Pardon me, sir (madam). Where is the levada to ... (the main road to ..., the footpath to ..., the way to ..., the bus stop)? Many thanks.

'Faz o favor, senhor (senhora). Onde é a levada para ... (a estrada para ..., a vereda para ..., o caminho para ..., a paragem)? Muito obrigado. (A woman says *muito obriga__da__*).

'**Fahz** oh fah-**vohr**, sehn-**yohr** (sehn-**yoh**-rah). **Ohn**-deh eh ah leh-**vah**-dah **pah**-rah ... (ah ish-**trah**-dah, ah veh-**ray**-dah, oh cah-**mee**-noh, ah **pah**-rah-jeng)? **Mween**-toh o-bree-**gah**-doh (oh-bree-**gah**-dah).

Possible answers (English/Portuguese/approximate pronunciation)

here, straight ahead, behind, to the right, to the left, above, below

aqui, em frente, atrás, a direita, a esquerda, em cima, em baixo

ah-**key**, sem-preh engh **frenght**, ah-**trahs**, ah deh-**ray**-tah, ah ish-**kehr**-dah, engh **see**-mah, engh **bigh**-joh

Try to get a native speaker (possibly someone at your hotel or your taxi driver) to help you learn to pronounce this well. You must also pronounce *very carefully* the name of your destination (see geographical index, page 133), because several places on the island have similar names.

When you have your mini-speech memorised, always ask the many questions you can concoct from it in such a way that a yes/no answer will result. *Never* ask an open-ended question such as 'Where is the main road?' and leave it at that! Unless you are actually standing on it, you will not understand the answer! Instead, ask the question and then suggest the most likely answer yourself, for example:

'Faz o favor, senhora. Onde é a estrada para Funchal? É sempre em frente? or *'Faz o favor, senhor. Onde é a Levada dos Tornos? É em cima a esquerda?*

If you go through your list of answers, you will eventually get a yes — with a vigorous nod of the head — and it will be a lot more reliable than just sign language.

An inexpensive phrase book, such as one of those published by Collins, Berlitz, or Penguin, is a very valuable aid, from which you may choose other 'key' phrases and answers.

It is always nice to greet people you may meet on your walks with a 'good morning' or 'good afternoon' (*bom dia/* bohm **dee**-ah) or (*boa tarde/*boah **tard**).

A country code for walkers and motorists

The experienced rambler is used to following a 'country code', but the tourist out for a lark may unwittingly cause damage, harm animals, and even endanger his own life. A code for behaviour is important wherever people are free to roam over the countryside, but doubly so on Madeira's rugged terrain. Please respect this country code.

- **Do not light fires.** Woods may be tinder dry. Make sure your cigarettes are completely extinguished.
- **Do not damage levadas.** Don't touch sluice gates or the stones used to control small sluices.
- **Protect all wild and cultivated plants.** Don't try to pick wild flowers or uproot saplings. They will die before you get them back to your hotel anyway. Leave them in place for others to enjoy. **Never cross cultivated land!**
- **Take all your litter back to the hotel with you.**
- **Do not frighten animals.** The animals on Madeira are *not tame* and *are not used to tourists*. By making loud noises, or trying to touch or photograph animals, you may cause them to run in fear — over a precipice.
- **Leave all gates as you find them.** Although you may not see any animals, the gates *do* have a purpose — generally to keep goats in — or out of — an area. Here again, animals have been killed by careless behaviour.
- **Walkers — DO NOT TAKE RISKS!** This is the most important point of all. Do not attempt walks beyond your capacity, and do not try to rock-climb — basalt crumbles. Do not wander off the paths we describe if there is any sign of mist falling or if it is late in the afternoon. *There is virtually no twilight on Madeira!* Nor are there any officially-recognised rescue services. **Do not walk alone**, and *always* tell a responsible person at your hotel or apartment *exactly* where you are going and at what time you plan to return. Remember, if you become lost or injure yourself, it may be a very long time before you are found. On any but a very short walk near to villages, be sure to carry with you a compass, whistle, torch, extra water and warm clothing — as well as some high-energy food, like chocolate.

Organisation of the walks

Our twenty-eight rambles are grouped in three general areas: the southeast; the northeast and the great peaks; the west and northwest. This is perhaps how you will get to know Madeira — starting out close to Funchal or Machico and then striking out farther and farther afield. We would encourage you to make a walk in *each* of these three areas, in order best to sample the island's landscapes.

We hope that the book is set out so that you can plan your walks easily — depending on how far you want to go, your abilities and equipment, the season, and what time you are willing to get up in the morning!

You might begin by considering the large fold-out touring map between pages 16 and 17. Here you can see at a glance the overall terrain, the extent of the levada network, main and secondary roads, and the orientation of the walking maps in the text. Flipping through the book, you'll see that there is at least one photograph for every walk.

Having selected one or two potential excursions from the map and the photographs, turn to the relevant walk. At the top of the page you will find planning information: distance/hours, grade, equipment, and how to get there by bus. If the grade and equipment specifications are beyond your scope, don't despair! *We always suggest at least one short version of each walk*, and in most cases these are far less demanding of agility and equipment!

When you are on your walk, you will find that the text begins with an introduction to the overall landscape and then quickly turns to a detailed description of the route itself. The large-scale maps (generally 1:40,000) have been specially annotated and, wherever possible, set out facing the walking notes. Times are given for reaching certain key checkpoints. Giving times is always tricky, because they depend on so many factors, but in fact the times we give are a little slower than those we actually make ourselves. **Note that they do not include any stops!** Allow extra time for picnics and other breaks, perhaps noting your own times in the margins.

Many of the symbols used on our walking maps are self-explanatory, but here is a key to the most important:

▬▬▬ correspond to roads and tracks on the pull-out touring map	▬▬ levada and levada tunnel	620 height (metres)
	●●●●	danger or vertigo
	↳ water/source	
	path of walk	♦♦† correspond to ✕♀✗ touring map
——— track or trail	- - - alternative	*P* picnics (page 12)
- - - - path or steps	best views	Ⓖ guide (page 34)

1 FUNCHAL · SOCORRIDOS RIVER (LEVADA DOS PIORNAIS) · VITÓRIA

NB: Roadworks will affect this walk; see STOP PRESS
Distance: 7.5km/4¾mi; 2¾h   MAP is on page 45
Grade: easy, but possibility of vertigo (10m/30ft drops on one side)
Equipment: stout shoes, sunhat, picnic, water
How to get there: any westbound bus to Reid's Hotel
Short walks (possibility of vertigo on both): Reid's to the Madeira Palacio (3.5km/2¼mi; 1¼h) or Madeira Palacio to Vitória (5km/3mi; 1¾h; take any westbound bus to the Madeira Palacio Hotel)
Photo references: see opposite. In our picture book, *Madeira* (1987 edition), see pages 17, 42, 62–63, 95

A 'citified' stroll with an astounding finish, at its best early in the morning or late in the afternoon — far too hot for midday. You stroll along a working, town levada. Babies are splashing in plastic tubs, while their mothers embroider tablecloths for the tourist shops in Funchal.

Start out on the Estrada Monumental (main road). Climb the hill, past the Quinta do Sol Hotel. Turn first left into the Camino da Casa Branca and then right up the Caminho da Nazaré. The levada is at your left, immediately beyond Nos 32-36 ('Pastelaria do Lagoa Azul'), but roadworks hide it. Walk along the roadworks for some 200m/yds; concrete steps at the left will take you down to the levada.

By **35min** you can see the Lido, banana fields and the tourist zone of western Funchal. Soon, behind a large housing development, you may experience some mild vertigo — to overcome it, just walk on the inside path of this double-channelled levada. Ten minutes later you get marvellous views of Cabo Girão and all the terraces on its eastern flanks. Then, by **1h** into the walk, at Amparo, two cobbled roads lead down to the EN215. At the second road, you must climb up a few paces to find the levada. (To join here for the short walk starting at the Madeira Palacio, climb the Caminho do Amparo for ten minutes to reach the levada — at your left, just before an electricity sub-station. From this point, deduct one hour from all times given below.)

Now you are just south of São Martinho church (see page 49), a landmark on so many island walks because of its especially graceful spire. Between here and the Socorridos there are several short stretches with unprotected drops of up to 10m/30ft; most of the time you can walk on the inside path. At **1h25min** pass a road leading up sharp right to São Martinho. Then, at **1h35min**, after a long cinderblock wall on the left, come to a road. At the right of the house below the electricity pylon opposite is the levada, *but it is covered by concrete*, as is usual in villages. In a moment or

42

two, a cobbled road joins. Follow it to a large house with decorative window tiles. At the left are steps to the levada.

At **1h45min** roadworks will probably bar your way. Best to head to Quebradas church and follow the road in front of it to the left. Ask for 'levada, Socorridos'. You'll rejoin the channel in the village, opposite a tap (drinking water). At **2h** a cobbled road branches off left, and then a cobbled *path* at **2h10min**, just before a level change in the levada. Now you're just five minutes from the breath-taking views at the end of the walk. You will return later to this cobbled path and follow it for two minutes down to Lombada, where you may find a bus. If not, stroll down to the EN215 at Vitória (by a marker, 'Câmara de Lobos 1km'). Here catch an eastbound bus, or walk on to the famous fishing village.

The glorious landscape at the end of the walk — the valley of the mighty Socorridos. You can picnic here in the eucalyptus grove (Picnic 1), but first venture just a bit further, to marvel at the golden curves and arching tunnels of this levada — sheer sculpture. . . .

2 CURRAL DAS FREIRAS · FAJÃ · FUNCHAL (LEVADA DO CURRAL E CASTELEJO)

Distance: 15km/9¼mi; 5¾h   **See STOP PRESS**

Grade: Ⓖ ; only for experts! Danger of vertigo throughout! Only suitable in dry weather; sometimes impassable due to landslides

Equipment: walking boots, long trousers, sunhat, cardigans, anorak, picnic, plastic bottle with water purifying tablets, walking stick, whistle, small hand towel (in case of emergency walking in levada!)

How to get there: 🚌 81 to Curral das Freiras
Depart Funchal 11.00 (Mon–Sat); arrive Curral 12.45
Depart Funchal 09.15 (Sundays, holidays); arrive Curral 10.30

Alternative walk: São Martinho to ruined Fajã and return (11km/6¾mi; 3¾h): stout shoes, sunhat, long-sleeved shirt, picnic, water; easy, but possibility of vertigo beyond Chamorra. 🚌 2, 8 or 9 (in front of São Lourenço Palace) to 'Moinho' (moh-een-yoh). It's the *first* stop past São Martinho church and is just past a mill (*moinho*). Cross the road to find the levada on the west side of the Caminho do Esmeraldo, just north of the post office. You'll reach Santo Amaro in 20-25min. Be sure to stay on the levada here: the main channel goes left in front of a very large building supplies depot. There is some possibility of vertigo after about 1h, past Chamorra, when the levada turns north into the Socorridos valley. At about 1h30min, watch for a steep path down left just *past* a solitary house: the levada path ahead is far too dangerous to navigate, but this path will lead you down to some lovely river pools and then up to the deserted hamlet of Fajã (reached in 2h)

Short walk: Take bus as for Alternative walk. Walk from the mill on the Caminho do Esmeraldo back to Funchal (see notes on page 50)

Photo references: see pages 46–49. In our picture book, *Madeira* (1987 edition), see pages 30–31, 37, 42, 54–55, 62–63, 90, 95, 106

To this walk above all the rest, we attribute our love of Madeira's landscapes and our insatiable appetite for discovering new watercourses. Years ago, having 'conquered' our first levada (from Choupana to Camacha), we decided to try another we'd heard of, from Curral to Funchal. Clad in shorts, sandals and optimism, and armed with a picnic, we set off despite the baleful looks from a farmer who followed us for some time, repeating '*má, má*' — a 'bad, bad' levada. At the end of the day, we escaped with only cuts, blisters — and sunstroke — as 'tangible' evidence of our excursion. But the memory of that walk lingered on — the astounding beauty of the valley and the few moments when we came very close to resting there, forever, in peace. To find and *record* a safe way through this paradise was a challenge that swiftly became a passion!

On leaving the bus at Curral church, **start the walk** by turning down right at the end of the square, then left, to find the post office. Pass it, and take the *first* cobbled steps down sharp right immediately beyond the public toilets (ie,

↑ 16 (Torrinhas),
↑ 4 (Pico Grande)

CURRAL DAS FREIRAS

700

680

550

550

randonnée 3

Eira do Serrado
1023

Curral de Baixo

950

900

700

600

550

EN 107

Danger! Two steep and slippery paths here are impassable in wet conditions. Danger of landslides!

randonnée 3 (Bôca dos Namorados)

450

550

900

Faja das Galinhas

950

500

350

Danger! Levada extremely narrow beside escarpment!

(Faja de Dentro)

②

800

700

600

550

400

250

250

200

Faja

Danger! Levada impassable beyond tunnel! Go into Faja and use the path to rejoin the levada beyond rock pools

600

500

maison isolée

450

EN 107

EN 105

Funchal, Monte →

Chamorra
350

400

300

Preces

250

EN 105

300

250

200

Caminho de Sto Antonio

Pico dos Barcelos
354

EN 203

② *danger!*

200

P
bosquet

②

Santo Amaro

Santo Amaro

Levada do Curral

Caminho do Pilar

moulin

Dr Barros

②

①

150

150

250

200

Lombada

Quebradas

Caminho do Esmeraldo

nouvelle route voir MISE A JOUR

Buxo

Virtudes

Dr Pita

hôpital

Câmara de Lobos

Vitória

100

100

Caminho de São Martinho

Martinho

200

São Martinho

Dr Pita

EN 215

stade

Dr Nuzzi

centre ville

Levada dos Piornais

①

Piornais

laiterie

Amparo
261

200

Levada dos Piornais

EN 215

200

150

100

gaz, fuel

Amparo

100

50

Madeira Palácio

50

Estrada Monumental

Lido

Reid's

50

N

0   1km   2km

Landscapes of Madeira 3/e © 1988   1mi

On a sunny day in January, Curral's levada is in full flow beneath chestnut trees. This is one of the very few places on this 'wild' levada where there is room to sit down and relax! It's a lovely picnic spot, overlooking Curral de Baixo on the opposite bank

do not cross over the river bed on the bridge). In three minutes the steps fork: go left, following the electricity wires. Soon cross a river bed on a concrete bridge. Then fork down right on a dirt path. Go down concrete steps beside the river bed and follow the path through fields, drawing always closer to the Ribeira do Curral. Soon you can see the levada channel below left, and you join it in **15min**, turning left.

Joy! This levada descends 310m/1000ft in its flow from Curral to Funchal, and the rushing water is always fresh and foaming. On every side, the majesty of the setting, the riots of flowers and orchards, and the bustling activities of the villagers compete for your attention. But always **stop** to admire the views, for the levada path is often **narrow and vertiginous right from the start of the walk**.

You'll pass through orchards of sweet chestnut trees, their ancient trunks towering above you like giant elephant legs in a dream-circus. After passing opposite Curral de Baixo (Lower Curral), in about **1h10min** walking, you'll meet a short tunnel below the Eira do Serrado lookout (no torch needed). Soon come to the grassy bank shown above, where

the levada makes a 90° turn left. Take a break here, to prepare for the worst walking on the route. Round the bend to find great desolate uncultivated chasms, reminding you once again of the river's torrent: its force cut the ravine cradling Curral das Freiras, for Curral is *not* a volcanic crater.

Five minutes past the grassy bank you'll pass a wooden gate. Now be especially alert: there are two places where you must leave the levada because it drops too steeply to walk along the channel. It's tempting to keep going until you find yourself in a very awkward position. So look out keenly for the 'paths' around these places where the water shoots down. **Utmost care is needed and please do not proceed if it looks as though there has been a recent landslide — or if conditions are too wet.** This part of the walk is manageable by expert walkers in suitable, dry conditions, and a walking stick helps.

The first deviation is five minutes past the wooden gate. Here a fallen tree *may* be blocking the path, but in any case be sure to turn down right, using a rough path across scree. You will rejoin the levada about 30m(yds) further on. Then pass through an iron gate, and **special care** will be needed to cross two areas prone to small landslides. If the path can not be safely crossed, you must **turn back here**. Just past the second landslide-prone stretch, and *about* **1h30min** into the walk, you must again leave the levada; there is no path beside it. Descend right down a steep path, which soon turns left round a bend. A waterfall and the onward-rushing levada can now be clearly seen. Rejoin the levada 50m/yds beyond the waterfall. Within a minute, another iron gate must be opened, and take the **utmost care for the next 100m(yds)**, where the narrow levada channel skirts an escarpment and there are very severe unprotected drops to the right. After you have gained the safety of a wider verge, by a ferny glen, you will be opposite the hamlet of Fajã das Galinhas, and you can marvel at its patchwork quilt of terraces flung over the hillsides all the way down to the river.

By **2h** you'll approach an abandoned farm at Fajã de Dentro. Five minutes later, the sound of rushing water alerts you to another drop in the levada, where you must again leave the channel. Don't take the first path down right, but the second (where three stone steps lead down). Two minutes later, you will have to leave the levada again for a short time, walking just beside it on a level path.

Pass a knoll with eucalyptus trees and you'll come to a series of steps in the levada channel, leading down towards the abandoned hamlet of Fajã. Keep a look out for the houses hidden beneath unruly vegetation below right, and look for the stones placed as steps, to lead you off the levada and into the hamlet. But for the moment continue along the levada (*provided the way looks safe and the railings are still secure*), into the wilderness grotto arching up left. You'll come to a long tunnel, pierced with many 'windows' to light your way and frame your photographs. Perhaps you will be as astonished as we were to find such an awesome place so close to Funchal! It is at Fajã, where the Ribeira da Lapa

Right: São Martinho Church, starting point for Alternative walk 2, and a landmark on many island walks because of its especially graceful spire. Below, opposite: Flowers spring optimistically from many corners and crevices along the vertiginous path bordering the Levada do Curral

joins the Ribeira do Curral, that the two become the Socorridos. When you consider that its flow cut this valley and today feeds four *major* levadas, you can perhaps imagine what a torrent it was when Zarco first saw it!

Don't attempt to go beyond the end of the tunnel! This is the place where we almost came to grief one winter's day years ago; we didn't know of the path through Fajã and continued on the levada, but it is far too dangerous to pass. Retrace your steps to the stones leading off the levada and follow the narrow and overgrown path into Fajã — perhaps to explore, perhaps to picnic, but certainly to ponder: *why* was this beautifully-situated hamlet deserted? And why so precipitously? (When we first discovered it in 1974, there was still crockery on tables and linen on beds in some of the deserted cottages!)

It can be a bit tricky to find the path down and round the dangerous part of the levada. Bear in mind that **you must not try to decend on any terraces!** Follow a path that skirts the village at the right, until you reach the lowest house *but one*, just past the second telephone pole. This was a fine, two-storey house; there are roof tiles stacked up by the front door. A path goes left in front of this property, and in just a couple of minutes it brings you down to another excellent picnic spot — the river pools, met in **3h** walking. As you sun yourself, you'll have a new — and less frightening — view of the rainwater cavern.

The steep path back up to the levada is through a woodland glen, and the walking is easy from now on, but just as rewarding! From the wilderness depths of the Curral ravine you emerge into the abundance of the Socorridos valley, its richness of colour and form defying description and photography. Banana and sugar cane plantations sweep down to the sea, creating an abstract painting in every shade of green, its crazy perspective caught in a frame of grape trellises and flowers.

Soon the now double-channelled levada passes Chamorra, crossing the Ribeira do Arvoredo in another woodland glen. At **4h15min** the levada turns east, and soon you'll reach Santo Amaro. Here the levada goes under a cobbled road: turn up slightly left and walk straight across, following the levada first past a shop/bar and then, almost immediately, forking left where it runs — after some 100m(yds) — between a stone wall and 2m/7ft palings, through which São Martinho church can be clearly seen. The latter part of this walk, in a Madeiran 'suburb', where every garden is a florist's display and even the daily laundry is put out to dry on bird-of-paradise bushes, is a treat for the eyes and a lift to the spirit!

You'll meet the crossing of the Caminho do Esmeraldo in about **4h45min.** (Here's where you join for the Alternative and Short walks; see page 44 for details.) You can either catch frequent orange 'town' buses here, or cross the road and walk downhill for one minute to find an old mill: a two-storey building with a blue lamp at the door and a millstone in front. The levada is just south of this building, at the left. Follow along until it forks; turn right here, passing the Pico do Buxo army barracks and following down many cobbled steps into Funchal. You'll have good views of the mountains up left, and a little-seen panorama of Funchal and the sea. In about 15 minutes from the mill (**5h** into the long walk), you'll reach the Caminho do Dr Barreto. Turn right down to the Caminho de São Martinho and cross to the south side of the road to await a town bus, or else turn left into the Caminho das Virtudes, following the signpost to Funchal and using our map to reach the EN215 just east of Reid's hotel (**5¾h**).

Walk 3: left, descending from Boca dos Namorados to Curral. The church is poised a mere 250 metres above the lower village! Right: climbing to the church through Curral's emerald-green terraces

3 CORTICEIRAS · BOCA DOS NAMORADOS · CURRAL DAS FREIRAS

Distance: 9.5km/6mi; 4h   **MAP is on page 54**

Grade: very strenuous. Steep ascents and descents, but not at all vertiginous or dangerous *at present* (although the path is slowly being ruined by children hurling down great logs they cut for firewood, thus breaking away the edge of the path and causing small landslides). The walk is unsuitable in wet conditions or in heavy mists, and an early morning start is recommended in hot weather

Equipment: sunhat, stout shoes (boots preferable), picnic, water, anorak, cardigans, whistle

How to get there: 🚌 96 to Corticeiras
Depart Funchal 07.00, 08.05, 09.00, 09.45, 10.45, 11.45, 12.15 and almost hourly thereafter; arrive Corticeiras 1h later
To return: 🚌 81: Depart Curral das Freiras 13.00 or 17.45 (only 17.45 Sundays and holidays); arrive Funchal 1¼h later

Short walk: Corticeiras to Boca dos Namorados and return: 4.5km 2¾mi; 1¾h; frequent return buses; strenuous; equipment as above

Photo references: see opposite. In *Madeira*, see pages 30, 31

H ere's the best walk into Curral for those of us who are energetic but suffer from vertigo. There are no sheer drops, and the well-engineered path is easy to follow.

Start out by leaving the bus at Corticeiras. Walk back downhill past the electricity substation. Ignore the first left by the station; take the *second* left, a few metres further on — a cobbled road leading up left. After 15 minutes, you'll reach the Quinta Mis Muchachos; here take the track swinging up left. It's an unrelenting, tiring climb of 300m/1000ft through dense eucalyptus forest from here to the 'Boca' (**1h**), but the views over Curral's setting are ample reward.

At the pass (*boca*), take the path leading down *left* off a track at the ridge, *following the telephone wires*. Soon the stony path dips into S-bends, affording excellent views of Curral's river, the levada course in Walk 2, and the tortuous motor road into the village. In **1h20min** meet a phone pole and the way becomes very grassy — almost mossy. Be sure to go sharp right at an S-bend here, and, throughout the descent, stay on the stony path, following the telephone wires.

In **1h35min** pass to the left of the knoll of Pico do Cedro, and 20 minutes later come to another grassy knoll with a chestnut orchard and eucalyptus grove — good picnic spots. By about **2h30min**, you meet the first cultivated *poios* and then your first houses, at Curral de Baixo. Here, be sure to go *left* up a stone path *before* the first house. For the next hour, you'll keep climbing and descending again, before you finally cross the bridge over the Ribeira do Curral at **3½h**. Take a break at the river pools before storming the citadel: 450 steps bring you to the levada; 500 more to Curral (**4h**).

4 CORTICEIRAS·PICO GRANDE·ENCUMEADA*

NB: Roadworks are in progress at the end of walk; see STOP PRESS

Distance: 14.5km/9mi; under 5¾h; *or* shorten the walk by starting at Boca da Corrida (see under Short walk below); **MAP is on page 54**

Grade: easy mountain walking as far as Boca do Cerro on a wide and grassy trail (see photo opposite). Further on, however, the path is narrow, often wet, and sometimes **impassable** below Pico Grande, due to landslides. Surefootedness is essential; **possibility of vertigo**

Equipment: walking boots, long trousers, 2 cardigans, anorak, sun-hat, whistle, picnic, plastic bottle and water purifying tablets

How to get there: 🚌96 to Corticeiras (see Walk 3, page 51)
To return: 🚌6 from Encumeada: departs 15.45; journey time 2h

Short walk: Boca da Corrida to Boca do Cerro and return *to Corticeiras* (9km/5½mi; 3½h). This is an easy mountain walk, but take equipment as above. To get there, take 🚌4, 6, 7, 96 or 107 *to Estreito*, where you will find a taxi. There is a fixed rate for the journey; it's high because the road is poor. (Note: some correspondents say there are now taxis at Corticieras, but don't rely on it!)

Photo references: see pages 26, 28, 50, 53, 102. In our picture book, *Madeira* (1987 edition), see pages 30, 51, 81, 122–125, 127

I f we were to choose our favourite mountain walk on the island, it might well be this one, which has so much to recommend it: proximity to Funchal and public transport, wide and easy, often grassy, paths — which very few people will find vertiginous, and magnificent views throughout.

Start out from the bus stop at Corticeiras (or, to save 90 minutes and avoid the only tiring climb on the route, take a taxi from *Estreito* to Boca da Corrida — see Short walk notes). From the bus stop, continue along the road the bus has just climbed. It goes steeply downhill and round a couple of bends. On reaching the Central da Pereira in eight minutes, turn right up the road to begin to climb 450m/1500ft to the forestry house at Boca da Corrida. You will pass through one of the island's most enchanting land-scapes, the aptly-named Jardim da Serra — garden of the mountain range. And the jewel of this market garden, lying smothered in orchards, is the lovely colonnaded *quinta* built in the 1800s by the English consul, Henry Veitch. From here he sent gifts of fruit and old wines to Napoleon when the *Northumberland* laid anchor in Funchal harbour on its passage to Elba.

You arrive at a forestry house at the end of the road (1½h). This is the pass of Boca da Corrida, from where there are wonderful views over Curral das Freiras. Head towards a double pair of concrete posts behind and to the right of the house. Turn up right *between* the right-hand posts, climbing sharply up a rough trail, heading for a fenced-in area. Soon

*or Curral; see description page 55

the route is very clear as it leads to the right of the fencing. After some eight minutes, the walk levels out to reveal the central mountain ridge towering above Curral. Soon reach a spot where a promontory on the right points directly to the grassy trail towards Pico Grande, so easily identified from all over the island because of the definite 'knob' on its summit. As the trail 'corkscrews' its way towards Pico Grande, be sure to avoid the crumbled old path down left to Serra de Água. Soon enjoy very fine views of Encumeada and the north, from the pass of Boca dos Corgos. Then, in **2h15min**, come to the first goat gate at Passo de Ares, from where you can look out west towards the vastness of the Paúl da Serra.

At **2h40min** reach a goat gate into the fourth pass, Boca do Cerro. *(From here, expert mountaineers, in the company of a guide, can climb to the summit of Pico Grande in fine weather.)* There is also a path from this pass down into Curral das Freiras; this route is described on page 55. The descent to Curral is an alternative walk if you find the way to Encumeada blocked by landslides past Boca do Cerro, but **be warned**: this path is extremely vertiginous in one place, with a corkscrew descent on narrow stone 'steps', and one of us, having sat down on the top 'step' to contemplate the abyss below, found that she could not go on — to the great disgust of the other, who could happily walk a tightrope between Arieiro and Ruivo. . . .

Past Boca do Cerro, our route (which was the main north/south trail over the island in the 1800s) is no longer

The old grassy trail corkscrews towards Pico Grande. The first part of this glorious mountain walk is easy and accessible to everyone. After you've enjoyed Picnic 4, why not venture along this far?

as wide and grassy. But it is easily discernible at the left of the gorse-bristling Cerro Pass — even if the signposts (to Encumeada and Curral) are broken. Turn down left, and soon skirt the awe-inspiring escarpment of Pico Grande. It will take twenty minutes to pass this rock face, where the **path is very narrow, wet, and prone to landslides.** Then the generally narrow route begins its descent to Encumeada.

In **3h30min**, past the Fenda do Ferreiro, reach a superb promontory with views all round, an idyllic picnic spot. In **4h05min**, there is a U-turn in the path, where you *may* see a sign pointing back to Estreito. Be sure to head northeast, and ignore a second path down left ten minutes further on

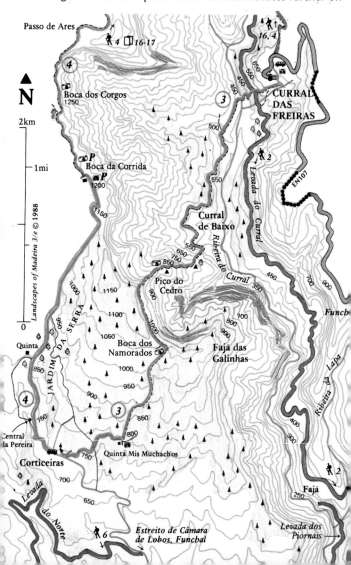

The valley of the Ribeira da Tábua, setting for Walk 5

(**4h15min**). Five minutes later, you will come into the enchanting valley of the Ribeira do Poço, emerald green and bright with *poios* and *palheiros*. Cross a grass-covered stone bridge at **4h30min**, and ignore two further paths down left (4h55min, 5h05min). Soon, at **5h25min**, you come to the pipe carrying water from the Levada do Norte (Walks 20–22) down to the power station at Serra de Água. Here, you'll have to clamber some 3m/yds up to the roadworks, which you follow to the EN104 (**5h35min**). Wait for the bus here, or walk down to the Vinháticos *pousada* (40min).

From Pico Grande
to Curral das Freiras   *Vinháticos*

Here's a description of the route from Boca do Cerro to Curral, pro-vided by Clive Scott (who is a very fast, sure-footed walker!): 'Past Boca do Cerro, our way to Curral turns up sharp right. As you pass through the gate at the top of the ridge, you lose sight of the Paúl da Serra and the Ribeira Brava valley. After fifteen minutes, pass through another gate and beyond you'll enjoy perhaps the island's finest view of the Curral valley. A 'J'-shaped outcrop is ahead of you, with Curral to its right and the road to Funchal climbing the far mountainside beyond. To your left you can pick out two bridges crossing the river, which itself points to Pico Ruivo. Every quarter hour the church bells waft chimes from Curral's hilltop church. Five minutes later you approach the 'J'-shaped outcrop, by des-cending a 'staircase' of stone some 3 metres/10 feet wide. [It will however appear to be only about 10 *inches* wide to those who suffer from vertigo. . . .] At the bottom of the 'staircase', turn left. The path, although steep and vertiginous, is always obvious, though perhaps covered in fallen leaves. It zigzags down to another gate (**3h40min** from Boca da Corrida). One of the river bridges is now below you, beyond a dozen or so red-tiled rooftops. You emerge from woodland to cultivation in a further twenty minutes; head for the bridge, which you should reach in ten minutes. Turn right on the far bank to climb to Curral, now about three-quarters of an hour away.' (Buses depart Curral 17.45 daily.)

5 CANDELÁRIA · TÁBUA · CORUJEIRA (LEVADA NOVA) · RIBEIRA BRAVA

Distance: 11km/6¾mi; under 3½h

Grade: easy, but steep ascents and descents; possibility of vertigo: this may be overcome by walking in the channel of the disused levada

Equipment: walking boots, long trousers, sunhat, cardigan, anorak, picnic, water

How to get there: 🚌 107 or 🚌 4 to Candelária
🚌 107: Depart Funchal 08.05; arrive Candelária 09.45
🚌 4: Depart Funchal 10.05 (Mon—Sat); arrive Candelária 11.45
To return: 🚌 4, 6, 7, or 107 from Ribeira Brava; if you take the early 🚌 107, you can catch 🚌 7 at 15.30; arrive Funchal 17.00

Short walk: From Corujeira as far as you like into the valley. Bus to Ribeira Brava and taxi to Corujeira. The road crosses the *very overgrown* levada 3.6km north of the EN101. Concrete steps at the left of the road, just before a large house, go down to the levada. Follow walk in reverse; return to Ribeira Brava on foot (or ask taxi to return)

Photo references: see page 55. In our picture book, *Madeira* (1987 edition), see pages 28—29, 104

Write iris, broom and sugar cane in springtime; straw ricks, sweet chestnut and blackberries in autumn. Take your pick of seasons to enjoy this fertile valley, graced with poplars, eucalyptus and mimosa the year round.

Ask the bus conductor for Candelária, which is the *third* stop after you round the point past the junction to Tábua. The second stop is at the Quinta Heidy; you get off at the *next paragem*. A few paces north of the stop, find stone steps leading up and *south* — by telephone wires. **To start the walk**, climb up here, reaching a house in **3min**. Here a dirt track joins. Follow it uphill until you come to an old stone trail at a crossroads (about **12min**). A chapel, hidden behind a house,

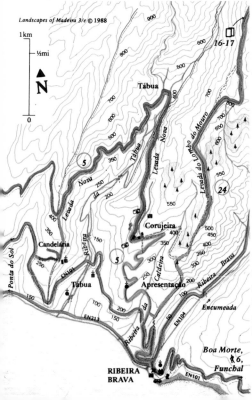

Landscapes of Madeira 3/e © 1988

is just east of this north/south trail (which climbs steeply
from the EN101 halfway up to the Paúl da Serra!). Turn
left (north) up the trail and climb it for about another 20
minutes, until you come to where it crosses the levada.
At your left will be a house and a wall, and some water may
be seen flowing into the levada on your right. However, the
flow soon ceases (this 'new' levada is no longer used — a
blessing in disguise, since you can walk in the levada channel
whenever the path becomes too narrow or vertiginous, *if
you are wearing boots!*).

Turn right onto the levada and head north to reach the
tiny hamlet of 'upper Tábua' — you'll be nearing it when
you pass through a sugar cane grove. You'll have to ford
two very wet spillways where the river crosses the levada: at
the second, you are in Tábua (**1h20min**).

Now head southeast in the valley and almost at once
you'll come to a new road. Here it's best to leave the levada
for some minutes; it's totally overgrown. Climb a few paces
to the track. Follow it to the right, crossing the levada and
going downhill for about five minutes. Leave the track just
before a sharp curve to the left, taking a cobbled path going
back up to the levada. You may hear the plop—plop—plop
of frogs diving for cover in the brackish water — you'll be
lucky to spot even one! The path soon improves, and the
best views of the valley are to come. After passing through
a cut in the basalt cliffs where stepping stones bridge the
levada, you come to the best lunch spot: here you'll sit on a
grassy verge where a gnarled fig tree arches over the path.
You'll overlook the river valley, its pools, poplars and straw-
ricks. It is in this area — the most beautiful — that the way
is also the most vertiginous.

Your senses will be assaulted by the perfume of mimosa,
heavy on the air, before you pass through a short tunnel
(no torch needed) and come into another valley. From here,
you reach another good lookout — over the coastal village
of Tábua (Tábua the Lower!). Soon pass a grassy knoll on
the right and then, at **2h10min**, concrete steps lead up left
to a large house. This is Corujeira, where a secondary road
heads down south to the EN101. Follow it down the
attractive valley of the Ribeira da Caldeira, coming into
Apresentação. Keeping straight down, meet the EN101 at
2h55min. Now you have a steep, but visually exciting,
descent into Ribeira Brava, 170m/560ft below. You'll
reach the esplanade in **3h20min** walking. On the way down,
you can identify Boa Morte's pine forest (Walk 6) on the
heights east of the Ribeira Brava Valley.

6 ESTREITO DE CÂMARA DE LOBOS · QUINTA GRANDE · CAMPANÁRIO · BOA MORTE (LEVADA DO NORTE) · BARREIRAS

Distance: 20.5km/12¾mi; 6h

Grade: level walking, but some narrow places throughout; **possibility of vertigo** between Caldeira and Campanário (sheer drops 70m/200ft)

Equipment: sunhat, stout shoes, cardigan, anorak, torch, picnic, water

How to get there: 🚌96 to levada crossing, north of Estreito Depart Funchal 07.00, 08.05, 09.00, 09.45, 10.45, 11.45, 12.15 and almost hourly thereafter; arrive Estreito 45min later; ask for 'Levada do Norte *paragem*'
To return from any point in the walk: take any bus travelling east along the EN101, such as 🚌4, 6, 7, 107 — check times in advance

Short walks: For *all* short walks, sunhat, stout shoes, picnic and water are recommended equipment, but **note possibilities of vertigo**

1   Estreito to the first waterhouse (5.5km/3½mi; under 1¾h)

2   Quinta Grande to Campanário (6km/3¾mi; 2¼h); this is not recommended for inexperienced walkers because of **possibility of vertigo** at several places along the route, where the path is narrow. Take any westbound bus to 'Ribeira da Quinta Grande *paragem*'

3   Boa Morte to Barreiras (6km/3¾mi; 2¼h). This walk is very easy. Take 🚌148 to Boa Morte: depart Funchal 13.00; arrive Boa Morte 14.20; *or* take an earlier bus to Ribeira Brava, from where you can catch a bus to Boa Morte at 11.10

Photo references: see pages 26, 61, 62. In our picture book, *Madeira* (1987 edition), see pages 28—29, 69, 79, 82—83, 88, 89, 91, 101, 124

All year round, this is a superb walk, with a sun-blessed aspect, through landscape rich in cultivation. Here in early autumn the grapes are harvested for some of Madeira's best known wines, and the valleys are thick with sugar cane and cherry trees.

When the bus roars up the hill at Estreito, you'll first pass the church and then a small chapel or shrine on the left. Just round the next bend is the bus stop, called 'Levada (do Norte)'. **The walk starts just here**, on the west side of the road, where you climb a few steps up to the levada (hidden under concrete — see Walk 1, page 42) and covered here by vine-bearing trellises. You'll hear it singing underfoot and reach the end of the covered walkway in **7min** at the most. Look left soon for good views of São Martinho church and, on a clear day, the Desertas. At about **20min** into the walk, be sure to look out for a path down and round a dangerous part of the levada. Soon you'll find yourself in the secret valley of the Ribeira da Caixa, smothered in cherry blossoms in spring — *do* be sure to try some Madeiran cherry wine (*ginjinha*) during your visit! For now, you might picnic near the abandoned stone cottage reached in **30min** or the bridge at the head of the valley (**50min**).

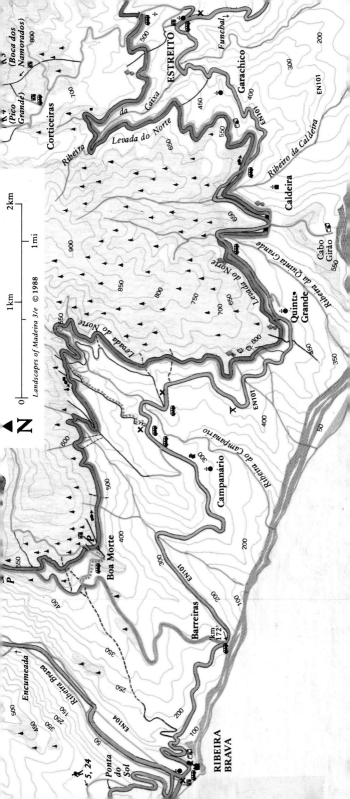

On leaving the valley, start counting churches to measure your progress! At **1h05min** here's the first, below at Garachico. A charming blue-and-white waterhouse is met at **1h 35min**. Its surrounds are generally locked. Walk to the front of the waterhouse, where you will meet a cobbled road, with cobbled steps inset into its west side. Climb these to regain the channel. In five minutes, cross the EN101. You may leave the walk here by taking any eastbound bus.

Staying on the levada, and drawing ever closer to Cabo Girão, enjoy the splendid views of the coast above Caldeira — its chapel doesn't count as a church! Just before reaching the tunnel at **1h55min**, some mild vertigo is possible as the first sheer drops are encountered. The tunnel is passed in three minutes and *can* be managed without a torch, since the path is very wide and the roof high. Now Cabo Girão has disappeared, and you're in the valley of the Quinta Grande river. At **2h10min** the levada skirts the river bridge below the EN101. Be sure to climb right up a dirt path here to reach and cross the main road, avoiding this vertiginous channel. (You join the levada here on the west side of the road for Short walk 2; deduct 2h10min from all times given below.)

At **2h20min** count the second church — at Quinta Grande — as you continue along another high and narrow stretch, above the EN101. Soon come to a spot that's exceptionally lovely in autumn: a riot of sugar cane and blackberries in a tangle below stately pillars of pine and sweet chestnut standing proud in iron-rich soil. The houses are festooned with dahlias and the aroma of wood fires is in the air. On rooftops, marrow and beans almost strangle the charming chimney-pots. The forest is alive with pink belladonna lilies.

Count the church of Campanário off to the west and start heading up the valley of the Ribeira do Campanário, golden with broom in spring. Soon you'll pass a small eucalyptus plantation, before reaching (at **2h55min**) some more severe drops to the left. The path is often only about a metre wide (some 2ft), with scrub at the edge and then drops of about 70m/200ft. Keep your eyes fixed on the levada channel, for it will take one full minute to navigate this spot. You'll pass more paths down left and then see the EN101 above Campanário — it has a very definite shape, a 'square' U-turn! At **3h20min** reach a lovely shady picnic spot, where the levada crosses the river at the head of the valley. Here the river sometimes rushes into the levada in a narrow concrete channel — a cooling sound on hot days.

Continue along in the wooded heights above Campanário, and in ten minutes (**3h30min**), you'll cross a dirt track. (If you're leaving the walk here, go straight down the track — do not take the left-hand fork. Descend gradually, first through a pine forest and later past many lovely houses, until you reach the EN101. Turn right at the main road to find the *paragem* — and an excellent local shop.)

Those continuing on the levada will pass a cobbled trail beside a first distribution centre and then reach another dirt track at **3h50min**. By **4h10min** a second distribution centre is met in the Boa Morte pine forest. The *levadeiro* here has created a charming garden of roses and dahlias; he's very proud of it — so *do* tell him it's '**mween**-toh boh-**nee**-toh'! The setting is exceptionally beautiful (see below), and the path is soft with pine needles. There are two dirt tracks down left into Boa Morte, before you meet the newly paved road into the village (**4h20min**). (If you are making the Short walk from Boa Morte, follow this road up to the levada

Stately pines reflected in the levada near Boa Morte (Picnic 6a)

Ribeira Brava's valley (see also page 26), setting for Picnic 6b

(10min), visiting first the forest and waterhouse (10min more); from here deduct 3h50min from times given below.)

After crossing the Boa Morte road, note the first dirt *track* left, reached at about **4h30min**. For the moment pass it by, and at **4h35min** into the long walk, look out over the lovely Ribeira Brava Valley, its terraces, poplars, and banana plantations. The views north and south are magnificent. This levada flows from far, far north of your present view-point — see Walk 20. *(Expert walkers may follow this very vertiginous, unprotected levada path north to the power station at Serra de Água — torch and boots required.)*

Now *return* to the track first passed at about 4h30min and descend gently, passing Boa Morte, all the way to the EN101. Resist the temptation to take either of the cobbled paths down right; once you reach the main road, you'll be able to see just how steep these descents would be. Always opt for the slightly longer, more gradual descent! When you reach the main road at Barreiras in just under **6h**, the bus stop is two minutes downhill right, by the sea. Catch any eastbound bus (or continue into Ribeira Brava 3km west).

Sun-burnished terraces of the lower Porto Novo (Walk/Picnic 8)

7 BABOSAS · PALHEIRO FERREIRO · LOMBO GRANDE (LEVADA DOS TORNOS) · GAULA

Distance: 19km/11¾mi; under 6½h   **MAP is on pages 70—71**

Grade: easy from Babosas to Camacha, but a steep climb to levada level; Ⓖ beyond Camacha — unprotected drops; **danger of vertigo!**

Equipment: stout shoes, long trousers, torch *for each person*, cardigan, sunhat, picnic, water, whistle, anorak outside summer

How to get there: 🚌 22 to Babosas, or 🚌 20 or 21 to Monte Bus 22 departs Funchal 07.45, 08.00 or 09.00; journey takes 20min
To return from Palheiro Ferreiro: 🚌 77: Departs from bus stop on the EN102 (beside the Levada Blandy) 17.30; 🚌 29 departs same stop 14.50 or 16.50. Both arrive Funchal 20min later. 🚌 26 departs from the village of Palheiro Ferreiro at 14.00 or 17.50; arrives Funchal 20min later
To return from Gaula: any bus (fairly frequent) travelling the EN101; if you catch 🚌 60 at Lombo Grande (dep 16.15), it saves 4km/1¼h

Short walks: For all short walks, we recommend stout shoes, sunhat, cardigan, picnic and water. Outside summer, wear long trousers and anorak as well. Here are three suggestions from many possibilities:

1 Babosas to Palheiro Ferreiro (6km/3¾mi; 2¼h); end the walk with a visit to the Blandy Estate (open 09.30—12.30 Mondays to Fridays — except holidays). Purchase tickets in advance at the Blandy Agency in Funchal, or they may be bought at the gate

2 Palheiro Ferreiro to Camacha (5km/3mi; 1¾h; *good* torch required); take 🚌 29 (frequent departures) and ask for 'Levada dos Tornos *paragem*, Palheiro Ferreiro', then use notes on page 65

3 Palheiro Ferreiro to Monte (6.5km/4mi; 2½h); take bus as for Short walk 2; perhaps 'fly' back to Funchal in a toboggan!

Photo references: see pages 20, 62, 64, 65, 75. In our picture book, *Madeira* (1987 edition), see pages 34—35, 46—47, 52, 56, 59, 68, 74—75, 78, 134—135, 139, 140, 141

F ollowing the sun-drenched levada path is almost like over-flying the south coast in a balloon. Enjoy the hustle and bustle of life at sea level from your peaceful eyrie!

Start the walk at Babosas Balcony overlooking the Curral dos Romeiros (Pilgrims' Corral). Follow the cobbled path down at the left side of the railed lookout. After descending part of the way down some cobbled steps reached in six minutes, you will come to a sharp right turn in the main path. We recommend that *all* walkers turn *right* here and follow the cobbled path. It will climb in zig-zag fashion (this is the only tiring part of the walk) up to the village of Romeiros (**25min**). Here, the levada is just up to your left. Pass the village shop (with a slanting flagpole on the wall) *and* the next three houses. You'll then see two short flights of concrete steps with iron railings. Climb up here and you are on top of the levada — which is covered by concrete (see page 42). Turn right and walk to the end of the village on the covered walkway; you'll soon see the levada in full flow, **40min** into the walk.

Curral dos Romeiros from the Tornos levada. The towers of Monte Church rise from the greenery. The chapel at the far right of the photograph is perched just above Babosas Balcony (Picnic 7a)

Whichever route you take*, you are now on Madeira's most important aqueduct, the Levada dos Tornos, inaugurated in 1966. Water collected in the north flows to the power station at Fajã da Nogueira (overlooked from Balcões — see pages 25 and 29), from where it is directed to more than 100,000 outlets between Funchal and Santa Cruz. This massive project includes 106km/66mi of main channels, with 16km/10mi of tunnels — see our large touring map.

Follow along the levada through pine groves, mimosa forests and an orchard, and at **1h15min** you'll come to a very pretty spot with lots of lilies, just before a cobbled road crosses. This is at the Quinta do Pomar (you'll see its tiny chapel over the road down right), one of the few places on the island where part of a major levada is enclosed in private land. Turn left up the road *just to the end of the quinta walls*. The path you want is the steep one here, up a flight

*(Expert walkers, who are accustomed to very sheer drops, may take an alternative route to the levada: after the stone steps 6min from Babosas, do not turn right, but go slightly left on the grassy path — frequently obstructed by fallen trees. You'll clear the pine and mimosa forest in about 6min and make a left turn into a narrow valley, with basalt cliffs towering up above. Climbing quite gently uphill, in 20min you'll reach the levada just where it leaves a very long tunnel from the north. Now you can walk along its path, but almost at once you come to a very sheer unprotected drop. From here the views are marvellous, but while walking be sure to concentrate on the path, for more severe drops will be encountered after you pass under the spillway diverting the Ribeira de João Gomes into the levada — now you know why the riverbed beside the market in Funchal is dry! You will enter Romeiros in 35min.)

of stone steps. Follow this path for a few minutes until you come to a fork, where a giant eucalyptus stands in the centre. Take the track to the *left* of the tree. In a few minutes you will come to a cobbled road (almost hidden at first by a stone wall); turn right and walk downhill for two minutes to find the levada on your left.

At **1h50min** you cross the EN201; then, at **2h15min** you cross the EN102 at the Levada dos Tornos *paragem* above Palheiro Ferreiro. (This is where you leave Bus 29 or 77 for Short walks 2 and 3: if you're making Short walk 2, deduct 2h15min from times given below; for Short walk 3, deduct the times given above *from* 2h15min.)

Just over the main road now is the setting shown in the photograph below. On the left is a smartly tiled cottage — it used to be thatched — with immaculately trimmed hedges, a garden, and a miniature orchard in front. Here you overlook Palheiro Ferreiro, the south coast, and the Desertas. The colours make you blink! The soil of the levada path is ochre-red, the house is pink one year, coral the next — and lilies run riots of orange and purple round the lot. We like to fantasise that it was from this cottage that the Count of Carvahal watched progress on his estate, which he named the Quinta 'do Palheiro Ferreiro' — 'of the blacksmith's thatched cottage'. (If you're leaving the walk here to return to Funchal, go back to the *paragem* just passed, to await the 29 or 77 bus. If you're going to visit the Blandy estate, the entrance is ten minutes downhill, opposite the EN201. After your visit, if you walk down the EN102 to the São Gonçalo road, you can catch one of the frequent local buses.)

If you are continuing on to Camacha or Gaula, you will come (**2h35min**) to a low tunnel, which it's best to pass through (there is no easy way round or over). *Watch your head!* Perhaps a long stick will help, too, for the path is very narrow. The tunnel is passed in ten minutes, and soon you come to various pleasant pine groves, where you may picnic.

One of our favourite places on the walk. At the left of this 'orchard' is the cottage that for us will always be the 'real' palheiro ferreiro!

After leaving Nogueira's pretty valley, you reach an impassable tunnel by a small distribution house. To its right, a fast-flowing levada courses south; to its left a steep dirt path leads up through a wooded hillside to a tall building. Climb up, making for the building, and then go to the track (or road) behind it. Turn right on this and, on reaching the crossing of the Caniço road (EN205), turn *left*. Then, one minute uphill go right at the 'stop' sign on the track (or road) into charming Ribeirinha. Pass the village shop on the right and continue until you see a white arrow signpost directing you back to the levada down right (along a dirt path which skirts private property for about five minutes). (You may leave the walk here — see Short walk 2 — by following this cobbled track up northeast into Camacha. The fifteen-minute climb affords splendid views down right over the Porto Novo Valley, graced by Gaula's church. You reach Camacha just by the delightful village square.)

By about **3h50min** into the walk, southeast of Camacha, after passing a house with a magnificent palm tree, you'll come to a short tunnel. Beyond this tunnel (3min to pass), there is a possibility of vertigo, for although the levada path is very adequate, there are no side railings, and the drops are very severe — perhaps 50m/150ft. Often waterfalls cascade onto the path as well, and you may get soaked, for you must walk slowly and carefully. Still, we hope that some of you will make this part of the walk — *with a guide* — for you are now in the lower part of the Porto Novo river valley (see also Walks 8 and 10), unquestionably one of the most beautiful on Madeira and the highlight of this walk. Heading north from Camacha, emerge from a short tunnel and suddenly waterfalls are singing everywhere. By **4h25min** you come to the splendid pools at the head of the valley, where a giant waterfall cascades into the river; all else is stillness. The best views are to be had after you head southeast. Now you can appreciate that it is like a giant amphitheatre, incredibly lush and sun-blessed. At Eastertime it is golden with broom.

Pass through the third and shortest tunnel, before skirting round the tunnel with 'windows' at about **4h50min**. Take a break anywhere along here, before you lose your views of the valley — but only picnic on uncultivated land! Soon reach a water catchment at Lombo Grande (**5h10min**). Just beyond it is the EN206. Turn right and descend gradually to the EN101 (about 1h20min walking — avoid the steep short-cuts!) — unless you are lucky enough to catch the No 60 bus which passes Lombo Grande at 16.15 daily.

8 CAMACHA · SALGADOS · ASSOMADA (LEVADA DO CANIÇO)

Distance: 6km/3¾mi; 2h20min   **MAP is on pages 70—71**

Grade: moderate, with a very steep descent of 250m/820ft to the levada. Surefootedness essential. **Possibility of vertigo** on levada

Equipment: stout shoes that grip on slippery, muddy surfaces, sunhat, cardigan, picnic, plastic bottle with water purifying tablets

How to get there: 🚌 29 to Camacha
Depart Funchal 08.00, 09.00, 10.00, 11.45, 13.30, 15.30; arrive Camacha 40min later
To return: any bus travelling west from Assomada along the EN101

Short walks: No vertigo on either; equipment as above, plus water

1   For those who don't mind steep ascents and descents, Camacha to the levada and return, via Salgados (3km/1¾mi *return*; under 1½h): the descent can be very slippery

2   Frequent 🚌 2 departures allow you to make a short walk from Assomada to a fine valley overlook and picnic spot (about 3km/1¾mi; 1h *return*. Ask for 'Assomada — igreja' (*igreja* = church and is pronounced 'ee-**gray**-jah'). Climb steps on west side of the church to join a dirt track. Pass an electricity substation in 8min and in 20min come to a *second* group of houses where the track swings left. Walk straight ahead between the houses to find the levada; turn right

Alternative walk: A path from the Levada do Caniço leads over to Gaula (see notes and map), affording combinations with Walk 7

Photo references: see pages 19, 62, 75. In our picture book, *Madeira* (1987 edition), see pages 45, 56, 59, 60, 68, 141

A ny season, any time of day, is suitable for this splendid walk in one of Madeira's most lush valleys. And this is a less vertiginous way to visit the lower Porto Novo valley than by making Walk 7; although the drops on this walk are quite severe, they are not as *sheer*, as there is generally scrub at the edge of the levada path.

To start the walk, make your way to the 'Centro de Saúde' (Health Centre) in the southeast corner of the village square (left of the café with the clock). Take the steep cobbled track heading south, at the left of the health centre. Keep downhill for ten minutes, until you come to a large school building (orientated north/south), where the track forks.

Crossing the Porto Novo (Walk 10): This valley is a wonderland of willow fields and houses all a-tilt up terraces edged with lilies, broom and daisies

67

Here go *left* on the lily-bordered cobbled path. This descends very steeply into the delightful 'perched' hamlet of Salgados, hidden in apple trees and decorated from top to toe with wickerwork. Part of the village is walled-in — peep over to see some enchanting gardens.

Keep on the same path, passing a tap on the right and, following electricity wires, go down stone 'steps' which take you all the way down to the Levada do Caniço (**35min**). Turn right to ramble to Assomada. Almost at once, you will see a path down left to a bridge over the river; the path on the other side leads up to Gaula (Walk 7). Soon you may notice a metal levada plate dated 1909. The 'feel' of this watercourse — its form, its rushing, laughing flow — is very reminiscent of the 'wild' Levada do Curral (Walk 2), built at about the same time. The only 'wild' spot on this walk is the narrow 'bridge' in the last side-valley; it's quickly crossed!

A particularly lovely promontory (see page 62) is met at **1h40min**, just past a grove of golden broom and a short tunnel. Here you may picnic nestled in sugar cane, 'santa maria', poppies and thistles as you overlook the valley, the south coast and the Desertas. If you're making the walk late in the day, the setting sun will paint the escarpment opposite the colour of burnished copper.

In well under two hours, a cement path crosses before a house. Turn down left to reach a dirt track in half a minute. Pass the electricity substation and follow down past fields festooned with nasturtiums until you reach Assomada's church and a short-cut to the main road in about **2h20min** walking. The bus stop is a few steps to the west, by a shop.

9 TERREIRO DA LUTA · MONTE · CHOUPANA · CAMACHA (LEVADA DOS TORNOS AND LEVADA DA SERRA)

Distance: 14km/8¾mi; 5h

Grade: easy, but some steep ascents and descents

Equipment: stout shoes, sunhat, cardigan, picnic, water

How to get there: 🚌 103 to Terreiro da Luta: dep 07.00, 13.30, 16.00; journey 35min. Or start from Monte (frequent departures)

To return: 🚌 29: dep Camacha 14.30 or 16.30; 40min to Funchal

Short walks: Take equipment as listed above

1 Terreiro da Luta to Monte or Babosas (1.5km/1mi; ½h); visit the monument to Nossa Senhora da Paz and enjoy the panorama of Curral dos Romeiros; buses (or toboggans) depart Monte frequently

2 Paradise Valley to Camacha (4.5km/2¾mi; under 2h); take 🚌 29 or 77 (departure times page 67): ask for 'Vale do Paraíso' (pronounced 'Val-yeh doh Pah-rah-ee-soh'). From the bus stop, head up the Poiso road (EN203) for 0.5km/under ½mi to find the levada

Photo references: see opposite and pages 64, 67, 75. In *Madeira* (1987 edition), see pages 34—35, 45, 46—47, 52, 56, 59, 94

S tately eucalyptus trees and the blossoms of Paradise Valley are our fondest memories of this walk, which **starts out** at the joining of the EN103 and the EN201 at Terreiro da Luta. At the left of the large building is a narrow and fast-flowing levada. Follow it all the way down to Monte, on a steep cobbled path beneath pine and mimosa.

In **20min** a cobbled road crosses, but keep straight on. This path will take you to Monte Church. After a visit, go down its front steps, turn left into a hairpin curve, then right down to the old Hotel Belmonte. Turn left here and follow the cobbled road to Babosas, passing a chapel up to your left. From Babosas use the notes on page 63 to go along the Levada dos Tornos to the Quinta do Pomar.

When you reach the crossroads with the chapel at the Quinta do Pomar (**1h55min**), turn left up the secondary road. You'll now leave the Levada dos Tornos and climb — rather steeply — up to the Levada da Serra 1km north. Stay on this road (don't fork left at the houses) until you reach the crossing of the lovely, dusty-red cobbled EN201 at Choupana. Facing you opposite is a steep track which you climb for under eight minutes, *until you see a short cobbled path on the right* leading to the levada (which is almost hidden in long grasses and somewhat hard to find at first!). You'll notice that for most of the time there's no water in the levada; it's been diverted to the Levada dos Tornos. But in summer months the hydrangeas and lilies are glorious.

Left: springtime in Paradise Valley (Walk 9, Picnic 9)

By **3h05min** you come to the Paradise Valley Quinta and then the EN203 to Poiso. (Here's where you join for Short walk 2, deducting 3h from times below.) Past here, you may picnic in the forest overlooking the setting on page 68. When you continue the walk, ignore the next track and road down right; the road you want will not be met until about **4h 45min**. Here a shop will be left and a wickerworks right. This road, running *parallel* to the EN102 below, takes you down to Camacha, just above the church (**5h**).

N

0   1km   2km

1mi

Landscapes of Madeira 3/e.© 1988

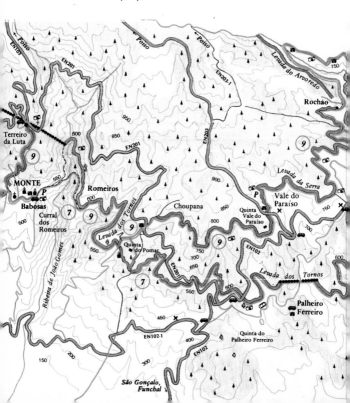

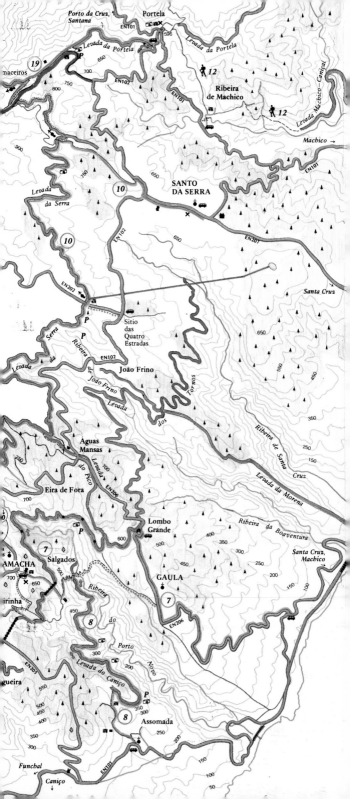

10 CAMACHA · JOÃO FRINO · SANTO DA SERRA (LEVADA DA SERRA)

Distance: 14km/8¾mi; 4¾h   **MAP is on pages 70—71**
Grade: easy, but there is a 13min climb to levada level
Equipment: stout shoes, cardigan, sunhat, picnic, water, anorak
How to get there: 🚌29 or 🚌77 to Camacha
🚌29: dep Funchal 08.00, 09.00, 10.00, 11.45 (Mon—Sat); dep 10.00 and 12.00 Sundays and holidays; arr Camacha 40min later
🚌77: dep Funchal 10.30; arr Camacha 11.15
To return: 🚌77: dep Santo da Serra 16.15; arr Funchal 17.50

Short walk: One of many possibilities is João Frino to Santo da Serra (5km/3mi; 1¾h). Take 🚌 77 to João Frino: depart Funchal 10.30; arrive 11.30. Ask for 'Sitio das Quatro Estradas' — the 'four roads place', where the EN202 to Poiso joins the EN102

Alternative walks: For the energetic, this walk is easily combined with Walk 19. You may go on to either Ribeiro Frio or Portela and find convenient return buses. Another interesting walk is from João Frino to Choupana or Monte; see notes for Walk 9

Photo references: see pages 67, 74 and below. In *Madeira* (1987 edition), see pages 2—3, 45, 56, 59, 80, 90, 120,121, 141

This is a lovely walk at any time of year, but perhaps the spring months are the most delightful. Then broom and gorse brighten the shady oak-lined levada paths, and the Porto Novo and Boaventura valleys are steeped in willow and wild flowers. Camacha and the pretty hamlets along the route are drenched in apple blossoms, and the levada is likely to be in full flow.

Start your walk behind the church, where the main road forks right to Santo da Serra. Take the cobbled road uphill to the left, keeping the walls of the Quinta das Almas on your left and taking the left-hand fork about 200m (yds) past the Quinta gate. In **13min** you will reach the crossing of the levada; a wickerworks is on your left and a village shop opposite. Turn right — a left leads to Choupana (Walk 9).

There is not much water in this part of the levada — it has been diverted to the Levada dos Tornos 1km south — but other delights abound as you watch the activities of the villagers. The levada has many about-turns, and each time you head southeast you get new views over the coast and the Desertas Islands.

At about **25min** into the walk, at Rochão, you lose the levada. Continue up the cobbled path, to cross a tarred road, and then follow the dirt track opposite, which descends to the left. This track (later a dirt road) *covers the levada* all the way round the Porto Novo Valley. In **45min** you come to the head of the valley, where you make a sharp U-turn. Follow the road out of the valley, until it turns away down right (to Eira de Fora); then you'll find the levada again, on your left, beside a house. (On our map, we have anticipated a minor tarred road which will eventually run from Rochão

The misty-grey flanks of the Santo da Serra range come into view

to Eira de Fora; it is shown in red on the map, with the levada omitted. At present, however, this road is very rough until you have rounded the U-turn, and not yet tarred.)

At **1h40min**, enjoy the rush of the Levada do Pico crossing your path, just before a track down to Águas Mansas. At **2h35min**, after passing the wide and pleasant Boaventura Valley, there's good picnicking above João Frino. Some ten minutes later, cross the EN202 to Poiso. (To join here for the short walk, climb ten minutes from the 'Sitio das Quatro Estradas' bus stop, deducting 2h35min from all times given below.) By **3h30min** you can see Santo da Serra and São Lourenço. Ten minutes later you get your first views of the north coast and the misty-grey flanks of the surrounding mountains, cloaked in dry heath trees. At **4h** meet a dirt track and, moments later, a waterhouse with charming gardens. (From here, you can link up to Walk 19 by following the levada to the next waterhouse, Lamaceiros, thirty minutes distant.) To end the walk at Santo da Serra, return to the track and turn left. Twenty-five minutes' descent takes you to the EN102; turn right, and then left on the EN207 into the village (**4h30min**).

Oaks arch over the levada near João Frino (Picnic 10)

11 EXPLORING SÃO LOURENÇO POINT

Distance: 10.5km/6½mi; 4h

Grade: easy

Equipment: stout shoes, sunhat, picnic, water, long-sleeved shirt in hot weather, cardigans and anorak with hood in cool weather

How to get there: 🚌 113 to Caniçal
Depart Funchal 09.00 or 11.15; pass Machico 10.05 or 12.20; arrive Caniçal 10.35 or 12.50
To return: 🚌 113
Depart Caniçal 14.00, 17.00, 18.00; arrive Funchal 1h35min later

Short walk: There is no suitable short walk from Caniçal, but a taxi will take you from the village to Abra Bay (Baía da Abra), from where you can picnic and ramble at leisure until the taxi returns

Photo references: see pages 21 and 76. In our picture book, *Madeira* (1987 edition), see pages 4, 18, 19, 108−109

S un-drenched São Lourenço Point is likely to be your first glimpse of Madeira from the air − doesn't it look inviting! You'll find that a day spent exploring this easternmost tip of the island provides a rewarding excursion for ramblers and picnickers of all ages.

Start the walk at the church in Caniçal, the end of the bus route. Stock up on picnic needs at a shop and then head out east on the rough road to the whaling station. *Don't* be disappointed by the beginning of this walk, which is not attractive. As soon as you reach the whaling station, just past a house and *before* a fenced-in garden on the right, turn up left to the main motor road. Almost at once, the outlook changes: ahead are lush green fields where cows graze, and, on a hill, the charming chapel to Our Lady of Mercy stands silhouetted against the sky. Beyond, the sun-browned arm of São Lourenço Point stretches langorously out to sea.

The first port of call will no doubt be Praínha beach, but you are likely to be disappointed here. More often than not there's no sand at all − let alone black sand! − for the heavy tides wash it away. A diversion up to the chapel is a better

Enjoy Picnic 7b here on the eastern side of the lower Porto Novo

way to use your energy than clambering down to Praínha and then back up again!

The road now curves round the knoll at Ponta do Rosto (where there is an airport radio tower); it's quite windy here. Be sure to make a stop at Ponta das Gaivotas, where you will see some crystallised rock formations. In fact, there are interesting strata all over São Lourenço, but the best examples are around this point, often called the 'fossil beds'.

When the motor road ends, you have reached lovely Abra Bay. Turn right down the track or climb up the knoll at the parking bay to get the best views. Find a good spot somewhere here to picnic, before you set out to enjoy some afternoon rambling/scrambling.

From your vantage point on the knoll, you'll quickly discern a path that heads up north towards a triangulation point. Following this path will take you to one of the island's most breath-taking viewpoints over the north coast. You'll be able to overlook the magnificent headlands as far west as São Jorge; but what is most astounding is the colour and shape of the rock formations below you: the lava rock seems almost fluorescent, so intense is its purple-red colour as it thrusts up from the emerald sea.

The nature of the rock makes it unsafe to scramble on the narrows here, beyond the end of the path, but you can safely follow another path heading south and slightly east. Head for the electricity wires, and when you reach the end of this southerly path, you will have exceptionally fine views of the lighthouse at the end of the point, the eyelet in the lighthouse rock, and the Desertas.

From here it's a half-hour walk back to the parking bay and a further hour and a half to Caniçal. If you've time, you may like to scramble elsewhere on the point; it's perfectly safe if you stay on the grassy paths, avoiding the rock!

From the path below the triangulation point: the rocks at sea seem almost fluorescent, so intense is their purple-red colour

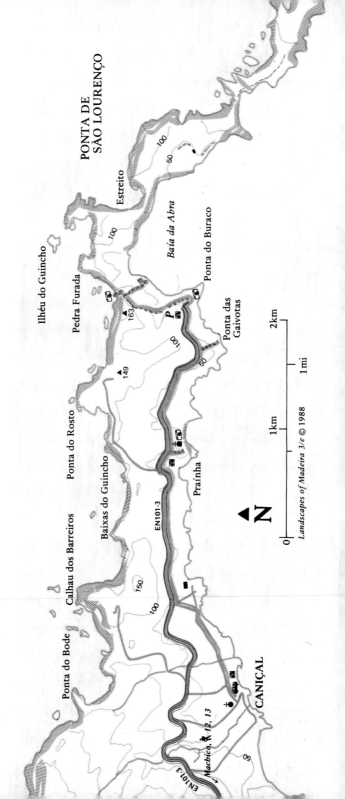

PONTA DE
SÃO LOURENÇO

Ilhéu do Guincho

Estreito

Pedra Furada

▲163

Baía da Abra

Ponta do Buraco

▲149

Ponta do Rosto

Ponta das Gaivotas

Calhau dos Barreiros

Baixas do Guincho

Ponta do Bode

EN101-3

Praínha

Landscapes of Madeira 3/e © 1988

N

0   1km   2km
    1mi

Machico, 12, 13

EN101-3

CANIÇAL

100

50

50

100

100

50

150

100

50

12 PORTELA TO PICO DO FACHO (LEVADA MACHICO—CANIÇAL)

Distance: 14km/8¾mi; 5h

Grade: easy on levada, but because of difficult descent from Portela, inexperienced walkers should perhaps explore the short walks *only*

Equipment: stout shoes (boots for descent from Portela), sunhat and long-sleeved shirt, anorak, cardigan, picnic, water

How to get there: 🚌 53 to Portela
Depart Funchal 10.00; arrive Portela 11.55 (Mon—Sat)
Depart Funchal 08.00; arrive Portela 09.55 (Sundays)
To return: 🚌 113: departs Pico do Facho bus stop 17.05, 18.05; arrive Funchal 1½h later

Short walks: All are easy and all start at the Caniçal tunnel; equipment as above (stout shoes will suffice); take 🚌 113 (departs Funchal 07.30, 09.00, 11.15 or 12.15 and arrives at Caniçal tunnel 1½h later); ask for 'Pico do Facho'

1 From the tunnel to the Ribeira Sêca *path* and the EN101-3 (5km/3mi; 1¾h): see notes for Short walk 2 below

2 From the tunnel all the way to Boca do Risco and return to the EN101-3 via Ribeira Sêca valley (see notes for Walk 13): 6.5km/4mi; about 2¾h. The path from the levada to Boca do Risco is met after 40min walking from the tunnel. Here stone steps cross the levada, leading up from a dirt track by a house. Follow the path up right; it's a ½h climb from here to Boca do Risco

3 Pico do Facho and return: the asphalt road to the peak is by the bus stop; 1h *return*

Photo references: see page 84 and below. In our picture book, *Madeira* (1987 edition), see pages 4, 58, 61, 64—65

The 'mimosa levada' offers an entrancing and easy walk, well within the reach of all visitors to Madeira. You can make it a very gentle stroll from the waterhouse at the tunnel entrance as far as you wish, or start on the heights of Portela.

The walk begins under the south-facing balcony of Portela's restaurant, on the 'old road' to Machico — now a track. Follow this track south for **20min**, until you reach the post office at Ribeira de Machico. Turn left here on a tarred road. When this tarred road swings left and uphill

The 'mimosa levada' irrigates the cornucopia of Machico's valley

in two minutes, go straight ahead downhill on a track, at the left of a large building. Follow this track now for some 18–20 minutes, after which it will swing sharp right to a farmhouse. Follow this right-hand curve round to the right. A few metres/yards into the turn, you will see a steep path at your left, opposite the house. It runs alongside an old narrow levada and follows the line of electricity wires. Turn left down this path and fork left some 10m/yds down. Then keep straight on downhill, always descending. In five minutes more, you'll cross a narrow levada 'bridge'. Over the 'bridge', bear left, but then continue immediately straight downhill on a very steep dirt path. You are heading for the solitary red-roofed mill in the riverbed, easily seen below, and you reach it in **1h** from Portela. Turn left at the mill and then take the first path down right. In a wonderland glen of willow and lilies, you'll find two old stone cottages standing guard at the source of the island's first 'new' levada (16km/10mi; 1949). Turn left onto it at the cottages and follow its flow through enchanting valleys.

You'll quickly gain the narrow Ribeira das Cales valley, a first glimpse of the gentle landscapes that make this walk such a delight. Past the village of Maroços, come into the splendid valley of the Ribeira Grande. From here until almost the end of the walk, there is little habitation, but the handiwork of the Madeiran farmer is all around. *Palheiros* dot the landscape here and there, mere specks of red and white in the great bowls of greenery reaching up to the sky. Perhaps you will meet a youngster bringing home a melon for dinner — he puts it into the levada and 'drives' his melon-boat with a stick . . . but it is more likely that your only companions will be full-throated frogs singing to their hearts' content.

A short tunnel is met at the end of this valley (**2h40min**; no torch needed) and then two waterhouses perched up beside the levada. Twenty minutes past the second, there is a good route down to Ribeira Sêca if you're pressed for time — just follow the light poles. The main walk continues by delving into the Ribeira da Noia, where it becomes obvious why we call this the 'mimosa levada'! All year round these golden trees will frame your photographs of the unforgettable valleys.

The great cornucopia of the valley of the Ribeira Sêca is reached all too soon. Linger a while beneath some oaks; there's a feast for the eyes all round you and the walk is drawing to an end. From here you can see bright Machico and the Desertas glimmering in the sun.

At about **3h25min** into the walk, soon after passing the narrow U-bend in the levada, you will notice stone steps crossing the channel. They come up from a dirt track by a house. This path leads north to Boca do Risco (Walk 13).

You'll reach the tunnel to Caniçal in just over **4h05min** walking, and you may end the walk here to catch an earlier bus. (Fast walkers may like to know that the levada continues *through* the tunnel for another 5km/3mi to Caniçal.)

But if you have time today, we'd suggest a visit to Pico do Facho; the asphalt road is just opposite the levada waterhouse at the tunnel. The views over Machico Bay and São Lourenço point are glorious in late afternoon from this easily-climbed peak. It's just 2km/1¼mi there and back; if you think you might miss the last bus from Caniçal (18.05), you can always walk from Pico do Facho to Machico and catch a later bus at 20.00.

Landscapes of Madeira 3/e © 1988

13 THE NORTH COAST PATH: RIBEIRA SÊCA · BOCA DO RISCO · PORTO DA CRUZ

Distance: 10km/6¼mi; 4h   **MAP is on pages 80—81**

Grade: easy climbing to Boca do Risco, but Ⓖ beyond: the north coast path is narrow, often slippery, and sometimes impassable due to landslides; unprotected drops of 350m/1150ft; danger of vertigo!

Equipment: stout shoes to Boca do Risco, boots beyond; sunhat, picnic, water, whistle, 2 cardigans, long trousers, anorak with hood

How to get there: 🚌 113 to 'Ribeira Sêca *paragem*'
Depart Funchal 09.00; arrive Ribeira Sêca 10.15
To return: 🚌 53
Depart Porto da Cruz 15.20 or 16.50; arrive Funchal 17.45 or 19.15
Sundays: only the 16.50 bus runs from Porto da Cruz

Alternative walk: Ⓖ; Porto da Cruz to Espigão Amarelo and return 10km/6¼mi; 4h). Equipment as above: *boots essential!* 🚌 53 to Porto da Cruz: dep Funchal 10.00 (*Sundays* 08.00); arr 2h20min later

Short walk: Ribeira Sêca up to Boca do Risco and return (6km/ 3¾mi; 2½h); 🚌 113 passes the Ribeira Sêca stop at 14.10, 17.10, 18.10, arriving Funchal 1½h later; stout shoes, cardigans, picnic, water. **NB:** see also Walk 12, Short walk 2, which visits Boca do Risco

Photo references: see below and pages 24, 78, 84. In our picture book, *Madeira* (1987 edition), see pages 4, 5, 32—33, 58, 64—65, 95

This is a walk of contrasts. Amble gently uphill in the Ribeira Sêca valley, marvelling at the sun-blessed fertility of Madeira's soil. You can forget for an hour what it has cost the islanders in toil, for there are few tiny terraces here, just lush farmland and fodder for cows. Ever so gently, climb always higher, until you reach the crest of the north coast. Here the wind — often chill — wakes you to the cruel realities of life on the island.

The north coast between Boca do Risco and Porto da Cruz is perhaps the quintessence of Madeira — nowhere else on the island can match its rugged, proud beauty in sunlight; few places in the world could match its harsh anger when lashed by storms. Here you cannot forget what it costs the islanders to survive.

It is not wise to walk the coastal path in winter, and *at any time* storm damage may cause landslides (generally between Boca do Risco and Espigão Amarelo), making the walk **impassable. Never** be foolish enough to attempt to cross

From Boca do Risco: The coastal path snakes its way eastwards

scree here! *Return to Boca do Risco*; perhaps explore Walk 12. Another day, you can make the Alternative walk (from Porto da Cruz — see page 82), to view the eastern headlands.

Begin the walk* at the Ribeira Sêca bus stop. Just around the sharp right-hand bend in the EN101-3, you will see a cobbled road to your left. Climb this for about **15min**, until you reach a three-storied house with balconies (on your left). Just opposite is a flight of steps. Climb these and turn left at the top, following a line of telegraph posts. You reach the Levada Machico—Caniçal in another fifteen

*You may also begin this walk at the Pico do Facho bus stop. Use notes and map for Walk 12, Short walk 2 (see page 78).

minutes. Cross the levada and continue on the good path to Boca do Risco.

The climb is quite gradual for most of the way, first up through farmland, where you will see many cowhouses and, likely as not, children carrying huge baskets of feed on their heads. Later brush and bilberry take over, leading to the great forests of pine and mimosa — and the climbing gets steeper. The air is delicious and fresh, with just a hint of salt blowing in from the sea. Within **1h15min** you will reach Boca do Risco. There is a cave here, just to the left of the path, where you may need to 'regroup' — catch your breath and put on a hood, if it's very windy. And ... wonder of wonders! You have reached a spot most tourists never visit, because it is completely inaccessible by road. Off across the sea to the northeast, you can see Porto Santo and its gleaming sands. The path is very good and level here, but the drop down to the sea is 350m/1150ft! Here are house-leeks like great cabbages, snowball trees, thistles, gorse, ferns, laurel, heath and wild flowers in every colour you can imagine. Turn left and start along the path to Porto da Cruz. By **2h** you pass through a gate and soon, looking east, you will enjoy your first views of Ilhéu do Guincho ('Screech Islet') — so called because the wind shrieks through its tiny eyelet. This is one of our favourite views on Madeira — dazzling in morning sun or glimmering in afternoon glow.

As you proceed west, new headlands come into view. By **2h30min** you'll reach a promontory just above Espigão Amarelo (the 'sharp yellow point'). There's a concrete post on the path here (marked JMG). It's a splendid spot for lunch, but there's only room for two or three!

After lunch, round one more headland before your first views of Porto da Cruz. Pass above Cova das Pedras, a beautiful semi-circular cove hardly visible from the cliffs. The character of the coastal path changes dramatically almost before you notice it, its starkness now softened by pine forests and banks of pink lilies. You look down to a sea of palest turquoise through pine trees standing tall in ochre-red soil. The waves break over the rocks below again and again and again, creating endless patterns of the finest lace.

About five minutes past Cova das Pedras and **3h05min** into the walk, the path leaves the cliff. Just 30m/yds past the narrow ridge between the sea and the valley, the way forks. Go left, descending into one of the loveliest valleys on the island, with its red soil, emerald crops, golden willows

Left: Terracotta finials look out from every rooftop. Here a bird watches over some terraces on the Levada Machico—Caniçal (Walk 12)

Cova da Roda (Walk/Picnic 17), one of Madeira's finest outlooks. In the distance, the coastal headlands stretch east to Ponta de São Lourenço. Porto da Cruz lies hidden near the sea, but the houses of São Roque bask in sunlight atop a 'lombo' and in the surrounding valleys. To the left, 'Eagle Rock' dominates the landscape. (Expert walkers may tackle the difficult and vertiginous path to its summit with a guide. The path begins at 'Cruz', not far west of Porto da Cruz)

and laden vines. Meet a dry levada and follow its channel to the right for ten minutes. When it heads right, turn down left, coming to steps and then a track. You reach an asphalt road, but this is *not* the bus route. Turn right to walk on into Porto da Cruz. By **4h**, after a long hairpin bend, you'll cross the Ribeira do Juncal. A cemetery is left and the church right. Go round the large building in the village centre and climb up left to the stop sign. Cross the main road to wait for the bus (which may make a 10-minute stop here if it's not running late).

14 QUEIMADAS · LEVADA DO CALDEIRÃO VERDE · SANTANA

Distance: 18km/11¼mi; 5¼h   **MAP is on reverse of touring map**

Grade: moderate; level *but slippery* levada path; **danger of vertigo throughout** (very severe drops on one side only, very adequately protected by sturdy railings, *but these sometimes come down in storms*); three tunnels (15min total); steep descent to Santana

Equipment: walking boots or stout shoes with *grip*, torch, sunhat, plastic rainhat, 2 cardigans, anorak, long trousers, picnic, plastic bottle with water purifying tablets, whistle

How to get there: 🚌 103 to Santana
Departs Funchal 07.00; arrives Santana 09.15; *taxi from Santana to Queimadas*
To return: 🚌 103: departs Santana 17.30; arrives Funchal 19.45

Short walk: No special equipment is needed to enjoy a day at beautiful Queimadas Park; just take a picnic and a couple of cardigans. Perhaps enjoy a bit of the long walk and then follow the levada to Pico das Pedras (3km/2mi *return*; 1¼h)

Photo references: see opposite and page 88. In our picture book, *Madeira* (1987 edition), see pages 22, 66—67, 72—73, 92—93, 96—97, 107, 132, 139

Think green. Think of rain forests . . . of emeralds. This is Queimadas — a mossy paradise even on the warmest day. And a bonus to this enchanting walk is a visit to Santana, without doubt one of Madeira's most picturesque villages.

Your route to Santana takes you via Monte and Terreiro da Luta up to the heights of Poiso. Here the bus will stop for a ten-minute break. Travelling with us on the bus once was a young fellow who had been on night duty at one of the Funchal hotels. Eager to practice his English, he introduced us to the 'working man's breakfast' — a glass of sweet Madeira wine and a warm hard-boiled egg. It truly set us up for the drop in temperature once the bus descended from Poiso down past Ribeiro Frio to the north coast! This chill will be noticeable even on warm days, and this is *not* a suitable walk for winter months; perhaps as much as 2m/80in of rain falls at Queimadas in winter!

By taxi, the uphill drive to the park takes about twenty minutes. On the way you will pass some of the very pretty thatched cottages for which Santana is famous. They are built in the 'old style', A-shaped and thatched right down to the ground, as a protection against the fierce northerlies.

When you arrive at Queimadas Park, you will find two charming *pousadas*. These resthouses are generally reserved for the use of government employees. But an overnight stay can sometimes be arranged (see page 36 — 'Where to stay').

Left: one of the charming rest houses at Queimadas Park

Begin the walk by passing the lower houses to find the old Levada do Caldeirão Verde. On your way you will discover yet another *pousada* — this one a miniature for the swans who live in the pools!

Moss is growing everywhere. It covers the levada paths and makes them *very* slippery at times. Every now and again, water tumbles down from above to cool you — unless you brought a rain hat!

The views are spectacular as you follow the levada westwards. After crossing two ravines, you come in about **1h** to the first tunnel. **Keep your head down!** Two more tunnels follow on immediately. Just before the second one, there is a path signed up the hills to 'Vale de Lapa', which would take you to a sunny patch of grass, superb for picnicking. Past the third tunnel, you will find yourself in one of the most remote parts of the island — wild with indigenous trees reputed to have survived the fires started by the early settlers to clear the land.

In about **1h30min** you will reach Caldeirão Verde. Here water shoots into the levada from a channel on the left, just before a river bed. Climb up the path at the left of the river bed and round a bend to see the wonderful waterfall (height 100m/330ft) and pool — perhaps picnicking here. Or, if you stay on the levada, crossing the river bed, you will come in a few minutes to our favourite picnic spot — a promontory in the sun overlooking the entire valley of the Ribeira Grande, 500m/1650ft below!

From this promontory, allow *at least* three and one-half hours to return to Santana on foot. Take the steep descent from Queimadas slowly! Turn right at the main road to reach the village; the bus leaves from the Relojoaria Freitas, near the church.

Left: From the strange basaltic rock called 'Homem em Pé' ('Man on Foot'; Picnic 15), the views are magnificent. Here the cleft of São Jorge's river slices through the fertile highlands west of Santana. Right: just one of the many waterfalls on the path of Walk 14

NB: Roadworks may interrupt this walk at any time; see **STOP PRESS**

Distance: 14km/8¾mi; under 6h   **MAP: see reverse of touring map**

Grade:Ⓖ; very strenuous, with many steep ascents and descents; unprotected drops; slippery; possibility of rain, mists and **landslides making the route impassable**; only **expert** mountain walkers should go without a guide; **danger of vertigo throughout**

Equipment: walking boots, rain gear, anorak, cardigans, long trousers, whistle, compass, sunhat, picnic, plastic bottle with purifying tablets

How to get there: 🚌 103 to Santana
Depart Funchal 07.00, 13.30*, 16.00*, 18.00; arr Santana 2¼h later
*except Sundays and holidays
Taxi from Santana to Achada do Teixeira
To return: 🚌 6: depart Encumeada 15.45; arrive Funchal 17.45, *or taxi from Encumeada or Vinháticos to Ribeira Brava for 18.35 bus*

Short walks: For both, wear stout shoes and take cardigans, anorak, sunhat, picnic, water; return by taxi for 🚌 103, departs 17.30
1   The short hike from Achada to Pico Ruivo on a new paved path (with shelters and two springs: 4.5km/2¾mi *return*; 2h) takes you takes you — literally and figuratively — to the high point of this walk!
2   From Achada along the motor road to the levada crossing 250m(yds) below the Pico das Pedras forestry house (6km/3¾mi; 2h); this may be combined with the Short walk page 87. Very easy

Photo references: see opposite and page 102. In our picture book, *Madeira* (1987 edition), see pages 22, 50–51, 66–67, 70, 107, 110 –111, 112–113, 114–115, 122–125, 130–133, 139

B lood red, then mauve; and finally silver and blue and gold. All was shadow; all was light. Nothing was real. Where sky ended and sea began, where mountains soared and clouds tiptoed down — all was merged into one. Sunrise at Pico Ruivo — the ultimate viewpoint on Madeira.

This is what you should aim for: an afternoon bus to Santana and taxi to Achada do Teixeira; an overnight stay at the recently-enlarged Pico Ruivo rest house; climb to the peak for sunrise; return to the *abrigo* for breakfast and *then* set out for Encumeada.

An alternative (and even longer) walk will be possible in the late 1980s, when the inn at Arieiro is completed. You will then be able to enjoy the sunrise at Arieiro (*with* a good breakfast, for the inn is planned to be run as an hotel, along the same lines as the Pousada dos Vinháticos). You can set out from Arieiro, following Walk 18 to Ruivo, and continue on to Encumeada (about 7 hours walking).

With existing bus connections (the morning 103 does not arrive at Santana until 09.15 — it could be 10.00 before you reach Achada by taxi — and the No 6 bus passes Encumeada at 15.45), you can only make this walk as a day trip from a Funchal hotel if you walk *quickly*, picnicking en route.

(If you miss the No 6 bus at Encumeada, you can telephone from the bar or from the Pousada dos Vinháticos 3km south for a Ribeira Brava taxi to take you there for a later bus.) Other alternatives are: *1* doing the walk in reverse, hoping for a lift at Achada; *2* staying overnight at the new pension in Santana (see **STOP PRESS**); or *3* arranging for a taxi to take you from your base to Achada for the sunrise.

However you plan to attack this expedition across the island's spine, we recommend it only for experienced walkers bursting with energy, and *only in summer months*. The less energetic can make the short walk to the summit and revel in all the splendour without the slog!

The drive on the EN101-5 from Santana takes you up to Pico das Pedras. This is a greenery devoted to experimental forestry and sheep farming. There are picnic tables and fire-places at the forestry house. About 250m(yds) below the house, by an old jeep track, the Levada do Caldeirão Verde meanders off west to Queimadas (see Walks 14 and 18) and east to Cova da Roda (Walk 17). Beyond here you will see the gnarled giant white heath trees that characterise this walk.

When you reach the parking bay at Achada do Teixeira, first walk to the northeast side of the car park (behind the house). From here you can look straight down on the valley of São Jorge; in the foreground just below, find the strange basaltic formation called 'Homem em Pé' — the 'Man on Foot' (so called because it looked like a cloaked figure to shepherds ascending the peaks from Queimadas). Now turn southeast and walk to the edge of the great cut: the third valley you see is the Metade (Walk 19, Short walk).

Then start the walk. Turn west and take the paved path to Ruivo. About **40min** up, you enjoy wonderful views of Arieiro, the Torres and the path of Walk 18. You'll pass two springs and three shelters on the way, before reaching the rest house at **45min.** Just before the house, the Arieiro path (Walk 18) comes in from the left. Take a break here (drinks and snacks available).

Five minutes above the house, you'll come to a red volcanic saddle and a sign ('Pico Ruivo à Encumeada/ cerca de 16km/←≪/vereda da D.T.M./1949'). At the left are steps to the Ruivo summit, and the twin lookouts are reached in eight minutes. You'll want to linger up here for quite a while to see how many landmarks you can dis-cern: the Torres and Torrinhas Pass, Pico Grande, the Paúl da Serra plateau, the valleys of the Metade and Curral, the Queimadas inns and valleys of São Jorge. . . . To the north-east lies Porto Santo, floating like a cloud on the horizon.

From the summit, return to the signpost at the saddle (1949/D.T.M. refers to the year that the Madeira Tourism Department took over maintenance of the path). Turn down left here and strike out for Encumeada. Once in a while, you may see a vertical or horizontal daub of white paint on a rock, but there is no other waymarking on this path, except just before and at Torrinhas Pass.

Twenty minutes below the saddle, reach a gate and, almost at once, the valley leading down to Curral opens up before you, and you can see the higher hamlet of Fajã dos Cardos. Most of the goat gates along the path are gravity-closing, *but be sure to secure those that aren't!* At **1h20min** into the walk the path forks; you will go left on stone steps, but first climb up slightly to the right, to see the fantastic views over the north coast, about 1300m/ 4250ft below! At **1h40min** come to a particularly good viewpoint down over Curral valley; just here, the path dips down left for a bit, before resuming its westerly course. At **1h35min** start climbing to skirt a cone-shaped peak on your right; this takes about 15 minutes — all the while you are enjoying the perfume of fresh mint and thyme crushed underfoot.

At **2h05min** you'll reach a promontory with chasms to the left. Here, a very poor path to Curral goes straight ahead; we go to the right. At **2h25min** climb down some steps and into another valley, from where you can see again the north coast. You may also discern an old path leading to São Jorge, just before Pico das Eirinhas. Already you can see across the great valley of the Ribeira Brava and São Vicente rivers, which splits the island in two. It's easy to identify the Ginjas waterhouse (Walks 20 and 23) and the new EN208 zigzagging up to the Paúl da Serra. Now the path winds endlessly, alternately giving views over the north and south of the island.

At **2h45min**, find a perfect promontory for lunch. Here two or three people can sit wedged in nature's rock-chairs and picnic while overlooking Curral das Freiras, the most southerly village below left. This is just before a fork in the path (marked by a red- and yellow-painted stone), where we turn *right* (Walk 16 turns left for Curral). Pass through an open gate and go down a few steps. Then the path turns left and descends steeply on worn stone steps beside a precipice, a **potentially dangerous** place, protected only by a meagre wire 'fence'. Stow away all unnecessary gear for this descent! Then reach a grassy verge overlooking the north coast — an ideal picnic spot for groups of walkers.

At **3h** into the walk you will be confronted by the first of *many* flights of steep stone steps. These lead up to Torrinhas Pass. Soon signs point the way to Curral (another path) and Encumeada. You may also see a sign pointing to the threadbare remains of the old (1800s) trail between Curral and Boaventura via Fajã do Penedo — see * opposite. If you have come this far without the interruption of road-works, the path now takes you over Pico do Jorge — forever up and forever down — almost an hour, on giant-sized steps.

Beyond a signposted spring (at **4h30min**), a rock arch frames your photographs of the valleys of Serra de Água and São Vicente. Then descend through a glen of giant ferns beside a basalt escarpment at Pico do Ferreiro. At **4h55min** you may see an arrow pointing to a steep path down left: part of the 1800s trail between Jardim da Serra and Encumeada, but no longer viable. *(Of all the paths radiating from the spine, only this route to Encumeada and the path from Torrinhas to Curral are used regularly. Expert mountain walkers may wish to tackle some of the others to the south or north of this walk, but this should only be done on the advice of, and in company with, a local guide.)*

If you are luckier than we are, this part of the walk west of Pico do Jorge can be glorious. But mists frequently descend by early afternoon, obscuring the valleys until you are well below 800m/2600ft. The mists will be welcome while you are climbing Pico do Jorge, and it is not difficult to follow the trail even in heavy mist and drizzle — but keep your wits about you and be just that bit *more* vigilant.

Whatever the weather, you won't fail to be delighted by the 'orchard' of wild lily of the valley trees and the blue-and blackberry bushes bordering the hundreds of stone steps on which you descend to the end of the walk.

By **5h50min** you reach the dirt track leading to the EN104 and the *miradouro*. Head south to find the blue and yellow sign to Folhadal beside the Levada do Norte, the starting point for Walks 20, 21 and 22. Wait here for the No 6 bus if you're in good time; it is hardly ever late. Should you think you've missed it, try to telephone a Ribeira Brava taxi from the bar at Encumeada, or else walk down 3km south to the Vinháticos *pousada*.

16 ACHADA DO TEIXEIRA · PICO RUIVO · TORRINHAS · CURRAL DAS FREIRAS

NB: Roadworks may interrupt this walk at any time; see STOP PRESS

Distance: 14km/8¾mi; under 6h   **MAP is on reverse of touring map**

Grade: Ⓖ ; the walk is strenuous, with a very steep descent. Sure-footedness is essential, and there is a possibility of vertigo

Equipment: as walk 15

How to get there: as walk 15

To return: 🚌 81 from Curral to Funchal; departs 17.45 daily

Short walk: as Walk 15

Alternative walk (only for adventurous, expert mountaineers): see *

Photo references: see pages 46—47, 88, 102. In our picture book, *Madeira* (1987 edition), see pages 30—31, 54, 132—133

To avoid that long slog over Pico do Jorge encountered on Walk 15, you can leave the east—west mountain ridge and make for Curral (or perhaps even Boaventura!*).

Start out by using the notes for Walk 15. When you come to the red- and yellow-painted stone (**2h45min**), where Walk 15 goes right, turn down *left* through the heath tree forest. Soon the descent affords simply magnificent views left to Ruivo, the Torres, Pico do Gato and Arieiro — they seem to tower close above you here.

About fifteen minutes down, it looks as if the path ends by an escarpment on the right; go into a deep U-turn to the left, crossing scree deposited by the Ribeira da Gomeira during one of its winter rages. Some thirty-five minutes down, pass through a gate; you may spot the old Lombo Grande path (passed at 2h05min, viability unknown) coming in from the left here. Now the way is beautifully grassy and shaded by sweet-smelling eucalyptus.

After descending for 1h50min (**4h35min**), you come to the first terraces. Cross a small levada and head left. Fifteen minutes later (**4h50min**) cross a bridge. Pass to the left of a second bridge in Fajã dos Cardos fifteen minutes later (bar/shop and tap). In another fifteen minutes, spot a bridge to the right and a path beyond it up to Boca do Cerro (Walk 4, Alternative walk). The final bridge is crossed 2h45min below Torrinhas (**5h30min**). Some 30m/yds below right, you'll see the Curral levada (Walk 2) taking its source in the Ribeira do Cidrão. The climb up 800 shallow steps to the village (**6h**) is, unfortunately, irksome in the extreme!

(*Expert walkers could tackle the path from Torrinhas to Fajã do Penedo, shown on our map. The route is still just about viable in summer months. Be warned, however: in the last years of this decade, roadworks are planned near the path, and it might become even more hazardous than it is at present. Go with a guide!)

17 PICO DAS PEDRAS·COVA DA RODA·LOMBO DO GALEGO · CRUZINHAS (OR FAIAL)

Distance: 10km/6¼mi; 4½h   MAP is on reverse of touring map

Grade: strenuous, with steep ascents and descents

Equipment: stout shoes (walking boots preferable), anorak, sunhat, cardigans, picnic, water, whistle, long trousers

How to get there: 🚌 53 to Faial*
Depart Funchal 10.00; arrive Faial 12.45
Taxi from Faial to Pico das Pedras
*If you *enjoy* getting up with the birds, you could take 🚌 103 to Santana (departs 07.00) and *taxi from Santana to Pico das Pedras or even Queimadas*, where you could do Walk 14 before this one!
To return: 🚌 103 from Cruzinhas: departs 18.15; arrives 19.45

Short walks: Two good short walks are possible:

1 Pico das Pedras to Queimadas and return: 25min each way. Easy level walking along a track beside the Levada do Caldeirão Verde. The levada is 250m(yds) below the Pico das Pedras forestry house. Turn left here (if coming from the forestry house)

2 Pico das Pedras to Cova da Roda and return: moderate; 3km/2mi; 1½h *return*. Wear very stout shoes or boots; take picnic, water. The walk is level for a time, but there is a steep, often slippery, descent to Cova da Roda — and a corresponding climb back up!

Alternatives: (1) Start at Queimadas; (2) Descend to Faial

Real slog: Start from Arieiro (Walk 18)! (Experts only)

Photo references: see pages 86 and 88. In our picture book, *Madeira* (1987 edition), see pages 26—27, 47, 66—67, 107, 139

Try to explore this walk in September — on a day when it's not too hot for the ups and downs to be too tiring, but when the hydrangeas are still in bloom. You might even be lucky enough to see them in October, because they bloom later here than those around Monte. Quite simply, the hydrangeas bordering the levada between Pico das Pedras and the path to Cova da Roda are the most spectacular on the island!

Start the walk 250m(yds) below the Pico das Pedras forestry house, where the EN101-5 crosses the Levada do Caldeirão Verde. Turn right (a left turn leads to Queimadas); you *may* still find here a sign for 'Faial'. Stroll beside the levada under the shade of holm oak, eucalyptus and a forest of gloriously-blue hydrangeas for **10min**, until the levada disappears. Here turn left down a twig- and leaf-strewn footpath, with the levada gurgling beside you. At the bottom, turn left on a track which shortly crosses some cultivated land (**35min**). You'll come to Cova da Roda in ten minutes (**45min**). There's a small cottage here, on the left. Just beyond it, the view of the coast is spectacular (see photograph on page 86) — a perfect picnic spot. The path goes on from here down to Faial, but we continue along it for only about 400m/yds more, to a crossing by a concrete water tank. Here turn off right. The track is earthen, but before long you will pick up the stone trail and descend to the first stone bridge (**1h35min**). Ten minutes later you get the best views of Eagle Rock (you may just toy with the idea of climbing it another day!), before descending into the next valley.

Pass through Lombo do Galego before bearing sharp right by a derelict house (with its roof at 'street level'). You pass its front door around the bend. A second stone bridge is met a couple of hundred metres (yards) downhill, just beyond a waterfall (**2h40min**). As you continue towards the next valley, do stop to admire the charm of all that is around you: the terracing and multi-coloured houses to your left, the mass of Eagle Rock in front — with the red roofs of houses clustered around its base, and the blue of the sea cupped on either side of it.

Another glen introduces the third bridge, and a further descent takes us to the fourth bridge at Fajã da Murta. Five minutes later we are at the fifth bridge (**4h**), which crosses the Ribeira Sêca — one of the three great streams flowing to Faial. From here it's a thirty-minute climb up the zig-zagging path to the hamlet of Cruzinhas, where we turn left at the electricity sub-station to meet the road.

(*Expert walkers, in summer months, and only in the company of a guide, can tackle vertiginous and claustrophobic routes around Fajã da Nogueira from Cruzinhas. They are shown on the large pull-out map. Behind the electricity substation in Cruzinhas is the (extremely vertiginous and hazardous) Levada das Cruzinhas, which may be followed to its source. From here you can either find the old (potentially hazardous) path up to the Levada do Furado (360m climb) on the other side of the road and go from there to Balcões, or you can walk up to the Fajã da Nogueira power station. From the power station it is possible to climb up to the Levada da Serra (335m). Walking with the current, you can follow this levada to the water conduit at the Pico da Fajã da Nogueira and then return to the power station. Or, walking against the current, you'll come to the 'Pico Ruivo tunnel'; this takes some 35min to pass — not for the claustrophobic!   Go down the stone steps (80m descent) in front of the tunnel exit, and they'll take you to the Levada do Caldeirão Verde. Turn right: Caldeirão Verde is reached (on your right) after some 30min and Queimadas 1h30min later. What you CANNOT do is link up the Levada da Serra and the Levada do Furado south of Pico da Fajã da Nogueira. We tried this once — another of our 'memorable experiences' on Madeira! The levada is completely crumbled away — see 'Madeira', pages 76-77).

18 THE HIGH PEAKS: PICO DO ARIEIRO ·
PICO RUIVO · QUEIMADAS · SANTANA

Distance: 16km/10mi; 6¼h   **MAP is on reverse of touring map**
Grade: exactly as Walk 15 — Ⓖ; NB: walk is sometimes impassable
Equipment: as Walk 15, plus torch and water

How to get there: *taxi* to Arieiro
To return: 🚌 103: Depart Santana 17.30; arrive Funchal 19.45

Short/Alternative walks (below): These are strenuous but not difficult; take picnic, water; wear stout shoes, sunhat, cardigan, anorak

Short walk: Go as far as you like on the main walk; your taxi will
wait for you

Alternative walk: Poiso to Arieiro (14km/8¾mi; under 5½h *return*).
This is an inexpensive way to see some of the island's most spectacu-
lar landscapes. 🚌 103 to Poiso: departs Funchal 07.00; arrives
Poiso 08.00; departs Poiso 18.45; arrives Funchal 19.45

Photo references: see opposite and pages 86, 88. In our picture
book, *Madeira* (1987 edition), see pages 6—7, 22, 66—67, 96—97,
107, 110, 111, 112—113, 114—115, 130—131, 132—133, 139

I f you're lashing out on a taxi from your hotel to get to
this walk — and you may have to, for there are no taxis to
be found at Poiso — then make it a *very* early morning start
and get to Arieiro at daybreak. The sun erupts like a ball of
fire; shards of light cascade mauve and golden over mountain-
tops and valleys. The mists clear quickly but reluctantly,
curling lovingly around the peaks, mere wisps and whispers
and then they're gone. A shepherd appears suddenly from
beneath a crest, shouldering a mighty load of firewood,
sending goats and sheep scurrying between light and shade,
as fluffy clouds throw shadows across the scrubby slopes.

Before setting out enjoy the views from Arieiro, Madeira's
third highest peak, far above the great ravines of the Curral
and Metade rivers. Most mornings the air is so clear that
you can see the heights above Porto Moniz.

Then start the walk by following the paved path behind
the hut. It's easy walking here, suitable for visitors with
stout shoes, but almost immediately you cross a very narrow
spine between two ravines. This is a hint of the great
chasms to follow on this trail linking the island's three
highest mountains. Built in the late 1960s, Madeira's most
famous mountain path is extremely well-engineered and the
difficult stretches are well-protected by sturdy iron railings,
opening up this glorious landscape to all visitors with the
right clothing and lots of stamina. But, alas, all too often
these railings are brought down by landslides, and there are
several dangerous passes on the walk. Use your judgement,
and **be prepared to turn back** at any point, if your way
ahead is not secure.

In **15min** you will reach the first viewpoint along the route. From here you can discern, to the northwest, a path running on the other side of the valley around the Torres mountain, the second highest on Madeira. The jagged teeth crowning this 'Peak of the Towers' hide Ruivo from your view for most of the walk, but after you climb up left past the first outlook, you *can* see the island's highest peak — and, on a clear day, the outskirts of Funchal — from the second viewpoint, reached in **25min**. In **30min** a steep descent on stone steps commences; at the end of this descent, a rock archway will frame your photographs.

Follow the path through the arch and soon look right to get splendid views over the Metade valley and the village of São Roque perched up on its *lombo* — the spine separating the valleys of the Metade and São Roque rivers.

The first tunnel is met in **45min**; it passes through Pico do Gato (Cat's Peak). Past this tunnel, a goat gate on the right leads to a crumbled-away path round the Torres. Be sure to go left on the well-worn way to Ruivo. Almost at once you will see a basalt rock face prone to landslides. A great slide here in 1981 obliterated the trail. If the fences are not in place, this is the most dangerous pass on the walk, often covered in scree. *Always be prepared to turn back!* If you can pass, stop for a moment and look west for superb views of Pico Grande (Walk 4). Then go on into the second tunnel at the end of the rock face (**1h**). The third and fourth tunnels follow on immediately. Just past the fourth, a grassy, broom-bedecked knoll commands spectacular views over Pico Grande and the expanse of the Paúl da Serra.

Enter the fifth and last tunnel in **1h15min**. At its exit, a path comes in from the right — the end of the derelict trail round Pico das Torres. Follow left on the Ruivo path, which now skirts a cliff-edge with some caves. Soon the way is very like the trail between Ruivo and Encumeada —

Starting out from Arieiro (setting for Picnic 18)

the broom gives way to gnarled heath trees which grace the sweeping vistas down to the Metade (see Walk 19).

It's a tiresome climb up to the rest house below Ruivo, reached in under **2h**, but you can buy a drink here before tackling the 10-minute hike to the summit. From here on, the walking is all downhill, beginning with a 45-minute descent to Achada. At the end of the paved path, continue by crossing the car park and going to the front of the rest-house. Walking past it, to the right, you'll soon have the view shown on page 88. Descend grassy steps to Homem em Pé, pass it on the right, and continue descending until you meet the road (25min). Follow the road downhill to the *miradouro*, from where the path continues (at the left side). After an hour's descent from Achada, go through a gate and soon reach the upper house in the storybook setting of Queimadas Park. From here there's another steep descent of 90 minutes to Santana. Turn right on the main road: the bus leaves from the Relojoaria Freitas, near the church.

19 RIBEIRO FRIO · LAMACEIROS · PORTELA (FURADO AND PORTELA LEVADAS)

Distance: 10km/6¼mi; 3½h   **MAP is on reverse of touring map**

Grade: only for the agile! **Danger of vertigo** (but the worst drops are well-protected by steel railings at present)

Equipment: walking boots or stout shoes that grip on slippery surfaces, long trousers, anorak, sunhat, cardigans, plastic bottle and water purifying tablets, picnic, whistle

How to get there: 🚌 103
Depart Funchal 07.00; arrive Ribeiro Frio 08.15
To return: 🚌 53: depart Portela 15.45 or 17.15; arrive Funchal 2h later (on Sundays only the 17.15 bus runs)

NB: If you've not visited it already, we suggest that you make the short walk to Balcões ('The Balconies') before setting out on the main walk: 2km/1¼mi; 40min *return*; see notes page 25

Short walk: Try to see some of the special landscape of this walk, perhaps going as far as the first steep drops on the levada (about 40min *return*). An easy short walk is the one to the Balconies: see **NB** above. Wear stout shoes, cardigan, sunhat. Funchal-bound buses pass at 14.30 (ex Sun/holidays) and 18.30 (daily)

Alternative walks: Take equipment as above

1 Do the walk in reverse, for handier bus connections (🚌 53 to Portela), but you'll have a very steep climb up to Lamaceiros

2 You may go to Camacha along the Levada da Serra: at the Lamaceiros waterhouse, keep on the levada until you meet another waterhouse in 30min. From there, use the notes for Walk 10 (in reverse). **See map pages 70—71.** Reckon under 7h walking

Photo references: see opposite and page 29. In our picture book, *Madeira* (1987 edition), see pages 2—3, 110, 111

T his is a walk to which we return again and again. The views are spectacular, and the steep drops add a touch of excitement! It's not dangerous if you have proper walking equipment and go carefully. But anyone can follow along with us for just a short way, to marvel at the play of light and shade over rocks and fountains, laurel and heath trees — this is what characterises the first part of the walk. Here and there stepping stones bridge the levada, and arches in the rocks above — you could hardly call them tunnels — entrance the photographer.

The second part of the walk — by pastureland, beyond the Lamaceiros waterhouse — is completely different, with sunlit panoramas of majestic mountains, proud valleys, and the tranquility of the north coast villages in the distance.

Begin the walk by leaving the bus at Ribeiro Frio and walking downhill past the stream until you see the blue and yellow sign to Portela on your right (further downhill, and on your left, is the signpost for Balcões). Here is the Levada do Furado, fresh and fast-flowing. It's very cool early in the

Opposite: play of light and shade on the fast-flowing Furado levada

morning; you're likely to need cardigans and anorak for the next hour. After **20min** you will come to the first steep drops on the left; anyone who finds the path difficult here should turn back, for worse drops will be encountered later.

In **25min** pass a tunnel on your right with a waterfall — a good place to collect water. In **55min** two fast-flowing streams course down left in channels, and a few minutes later some of the best photos may be had, where stepping stones bridge the levada and the play of light and shade is intensified. Come to a large grassy verge in **1h10min**. From here you can see the terraces to the north coast. Between this verge and Pico do Suna, there are some *very sharp* U-turns in the levada. In most cases, it is easier to walk across the river bed than to follow the levada path.

At about **2h** you will pass through a cleft in the rock. Turning left, you can climb a path which doubles back over the levada and climbs Pico do Suna (reached in about 15 minutes and offering very fine views). Ten minutes past this cleft, below the Suna peak, you pass a very narrow part of the levada at a precipice. The railings here are *sometimes* in a state of disrepair; if so, go with the utmost care for the next several minutes!

By **2h20min** you'll reach the Lamaceiros waterhouse and look out east to São Lourenço. About 30m(yds) past the waterhouse turn left down a path to find the narrow Levada da Portela. Follow it to a forestry house, and here join roadworks at the right. Descend gently and enjoy the most marvellous views imaginable of Faial, Penha de Águia and Porto da Cruz. When the levada disappears, stay on the road. Some 130m/yds below, go left on a grassy path to find the levada left and fenced-in pastureland right. At a fork, climb the grass path to the right. Follow the levada, the pastureland at your right, and you'll come to a waterhouse. Go left here, down to the EN102. Portela's restaurant is downhill left; catch the bus opposite the shops south of it, *on the EN101.*

The giant waterfall on the Levada das Rabaças, just before the short tunnel reached in 35 minutes (Picnic 22)

20 ENCUMEADA · GINJAS WATERHOUSE (LEVADA DO NORTE) · FEITEIRAS

Distance: 13km/7½mi; 4½h   **MAP is on reverse of touring map**

Grade: level walking on good, wide levada path; gradual, but *very long* descent (EN208) to Feiteiras. **Possibility of vertigo** and four long tunnels (35min in all). Walk is sometimes awash and impassable

Equipment: walking boots, torch, whistle, sunhat, long trousers, 2 cardigans, anorak, picnic, plastic bottle with water purifying tablets

How to get there: 🚌6 to Encumeada
Depart Funchal 07.30; arrive Encumeada 09.40
To return: 🚌6: depart Feiteiras 15.15; arrive Funchal 17.45

Short walks: For the first, you will need only stout shoes, sunhat, and a picnic; for the second, all the equipment listed above is required. Both return to Encumeada; 🚌6 passes here at 15.45 and arrives Funchal 17.45

1 Encumeada to the giant waterfall (3.5km/2¼mi; 1¼h *return*; **possibility of vertigo**). Do *not* turn right into the tunnel at 14min

2 Encumeada to Folhadal (6km/3¾mi; 2h *return*; **possibility of vertigo**). At Folhadal you will have splendid views of Ruivo and the valley leading to São Vicente, as well as the Folhadal waterfalls

NB: See also Walks 4, 21—24, and STOP PRESS

Photo references: see opposite and pages 26, 28, 104, 107. In our picture book, *Madeira* (1987 edition), see pages 50—51, 57, 70—71, 89, 107, 122—123, 124—125, 126, 128—129

Power and majesty. These may be your first impressions when you step onto the levada at Encumeada Pass. You are at the centre of the deep north-south cleft that splits the island. To the east rise the great peaks; to the south lies the magnificent valley of Serra de Água. And at your feet, the Levada do Norte, 1m/3ft wide and just as deep, surges along its course in a massive concrete channel.

Enjoy the early morning views of Câmara de Lobos and then the Ribeira Brava valley, as you climb the EN104. Ten minutes before reaching Encumeada, you will pass the Pousada dos Vinháticos — *do* try to spend a night or two here; the hotel is excellently situated for walkers.

When the bus reaches Encumeada, the levada is just a few steps up from the road, opposite the bar, on the south side of the pass. **Start the walk** by following along west, and you'll be amazed by the abundance of vegetation: conifers of every description, heath and hawthorn, with a tangle of laurel, azaleas, hydrangeas, lilies and myriad wild flowers. If you're lucky enough to come in June, you'll see the splendid cornflower-blue Pride of Madeira in all its glory. In **12min** you come to the promontory of Lapa do Galho, from where you will get the best views down over the valley and the south coast. Contrast this lush golden sweep with São Vicente's emerald hillsides seen later in the walk.

From here you can also see the levada continuing to the east and emptying into the metal pipe in which the water is funnelled down to the power station (1953). There are 50km/31mi of channels north of here (including 11km/7mi of tunnels). From the power station the water flows on in another 35km/22mi of channels (7km/4½mi of tunnels) to irrigate the fields of Ribeira Brava and Câmara de Lobos — see Walk 6, page 58.

Two minutes past the promontory the levada forks; turn right into the tunnel (or keep left for Short walk 1). We'll never forget our first walk here. It was a brilliantly sunny, warm day. We approached the tunnel to find what seemed a washing-machine gone mad — thick white foam was pouring from it! It was fog, rushing through from the other side. If you arrive to find this fog, it doesn't bode well for your walk and probably means that, at least until you begin the descent into Feiteiras, you will not see much. You may decide to combine Short walk 1 with a visit to the charming valley of the Ribeira do Poço (see page 55, Walk 4).

You can collect water from the sluice just to your right before entering the tunnel (10min to pass). At **25min** you are out of the tunnel. Already you have your first views of the north coast. In another 10 minutes you'll come to a very short tunnel through which you may photograph another sluice falls. The second, longest tunnel, looms at **40min**; you can also collect water here, from the falls at the left. The tunnel is straight ahead of you, with a workmen's cave at its right. It looks too low to pass, but you will find on entering that you can stand straight up in it. It will take 15 minutes to pass, and well before you reach the end, you will hear what sounds like a train rushing towards you! The roar is made by the water from the Folhadal falls, surging into the levada over a sluice at the end of the tunnel.

Look left as you leave the tunnel to see the two great waterfalls of Folhadal pouring down a rock-face in this wilderness basin. On your right there are excellent views of the peaks — the jagged Torres being most obvious. You also have a view of the enchanting valley leading past Rosário to São Vicente — all too fleeting, for at **1h15min** you reach the third tunnel (5min to pass); exit and right on into the fourth and last tunnel (5min). After this last tunnel, at **1h25min** into the walk, the views down to the north coast and to the peaks are really best, but here are also the first steep drops, and those who suffer from vertigo *may* have difficulty, although the path is very adequate.

There's also a very short tunnel here (no torch needed) and then a grassy verge where you could picnic and hang your legs out over eternity! This is just before you meet the Ginjas waterhouse at **1h30min**. Behind the waterhouse is the new EN208. Although it has obliterated a centuries-old trail and, frankly, ruined the end of this walk, we must grudgingly admit that it will be a spectacular drive for those people who tour by car — for preference or necessity.

Indeed, the *frenzy* of road-building going on all over the island means that several of our walks may not be so enjoyable during the latter half of this decade, and alas, some lovely old moss-covered trails are lost forever. But at least the sound of bulldozers will cease eventually, and it is unlikely that these roads will ever be heavily used; by the 1990s, all should again be still at Encumeada, on the Paúl da Serra — and here at the Ginjas waterhouse, from where you can listen to the carillon of Nossa Senhora da Fâtima on the eastern hillside south of the village of São Vicente.

Left: on the path of Walk 15. From this vantage point, there's a new view of Pico Grande, highlighting its massive and austere escarpment

After lunch, remember to allow about 2h30min for the 7.7km/4¾mi descent to Feiteiras along the endlessly-winding road. Perhaps you'll be lucky enough to be offered a lift!

Along the route, by Ginjas, the farms and *palheiros* are rustic and unpainted — a mellow backdrop to the brilliance of the flowers. At Feiteiras, there's a shortcut to the main road, where a narrow levada crosses by cobbled steps covered with vine trellises. Keep the levada on your left until it shoots into a vertical pipe; continue down the steps, crossing the asphalt secondary road *twice* to reach the EN104 (opposite a very large and elegant house, with two sets of stairs at the front).

21 ENCUMEADA · PICO REDONDO · POUSADA DOS VINHÁTICOS

Distance: 4km/2½mi; 1¾h   **MAP is on reverse of touring map**

Grade: fairly easy, but only recommended for dry weather; the steep path leading to Pico Redondo would be hazardous when wet

Equipment: stout shoes or walking boots, sunhat, long trousers, whistle, cardigan, anorak, picnic, water

How to get there: 🚌 6 to Encumeada
Depart Funchal 07.30; arrive Encumeada 09.40
To return: 🚌 6: departs Vinháticos 15.55; arrives Funchal 17.45

Short walk: Follow the main walk for about 25min — until you find a good picnic spot on the ridge connecting the levada to Pico Redondo. Grade and equipment as above; about 2km *return*

Photo references: see opposite and pages 26, 28. In our picture book, *Madeira* (1987 edition), see pages 50—51, 70, 122—123, 124—125, 126, 128

The grass on Pico Redondo is just as soft and green — or in summer and autumn as golden — as it looks every time you walk west on the Levada do Norte and pass this inviting knoll. It's about time to enjoy a picnic here!

Start out as in Walk 20 (page 101), coming in **14min** to the first tunnel. Keep left on the levada and in five minutes find the path out left to Pico Redondo, half hidden in broom trees. Hold on to the trees while making this steep descent! The path goes straight out to the peak — although it's often masked by fallen trees and ferns. You'll come to a fence in about **50min**. *Do not damage the fence!* Find a place where you can clamber over with the help of friends. You'll be up with the sheep, at the top of the knoll, in under **1h**. What a lovely, grassy place to stretch out and watch clouds roll by!

When it's time to leave, return to the fence and *follow it* (without climbing it) back towards the levada. Soon you'll see a gate off to the left (southwest, downhill). Make for this gate, on another hard-to-find path. *Close the gate behind you;* it's done up with both a catch and wire. Beyond the gate, the path heads downhill, but soon goes left. Come to a T-fork in about 15min and go right to a cow house, where you take a sharp left. Zig-zag through freshly-cultivated plots to reach and cross a very narrow levada. The path drops down on 'steps' beside this levada; once at the foot of the steps, find it again, heading left. Ten minutes past the levada crossing, fork right alongside a pipe, to cross another narrow levada in two minutes. Follow the narrow path at the right of this levada all the way to the EN104 at the north side of the Vinháticos *pousada* (50min from the gate at Pico Redondo). What better spot to end a walk?

Left: On a stormy day, a sun-shaft alights on Pico Redondo

22 ENCUMEADA· CASCALHO· ENCUMEADA (LEVADAS DO NORTE AND RABAÇAS)

See STOP PRESS

Distance: 11km/6¾mi; 4h   **MAP is on reverse of touring map**

Grade: Ⓖ; a summer walk for experts only! Vertiginous walking along narrow levada paths, many of them unprotected, and at least two potentially hazardous scree areas; two tunnels (one very long)

Equipment: walking boots, long trousers, good torch *for each member of the party*, whistle, sunhat, plastic bottle with water purifying tablets, picnic, 2 cardigans, anorak, rainhat

How to get there: 🚌 6 to Encumeada
Depart Funchal 07.30; arrive Encumeada 09.40
To return: 🚌 6: dep Encumeada 15.45; arr Funchal 17.45

Short walk: To the waterhouse (5km/3mi; 1¾h *return*). No guide necessary; **possibility of vertigo**; stout shoes, sunhat, picnic, water

Photo references: see opposite and pages 26, 28, 100, 104. In *Madeira*, see pages 50—51, 70, 84—85, 100, 122—123, 124—125, 126

C ascalho is a primeval wonderland, known only to goats, levada-builders and a very, very few guides and walkers. It's a hidden bowl of waterfalls where the Ribeira da Ponta do Sol gathered its strength; the torrent now feeds the Levada das Rabaças (1970). If you have the right equipment and are an *expert* walker with a head for heights, *now* is the time to make this walk, for the most dangerous parts of the levada path are still protected by railings left by the levada builders; once they come down, they may not be replaced.

The path of the walk is simplicity itself: **start out** as in Walk 20, but stay on the open levada to pass the waterfall (see page 100; **35min**). Two minutes later come to a short tunnel (3min), and then look down onto the Pousada dos Vinháticos — but you may find the path quite vertiginous here. Pass the levada keeper's lonely 'house' at **50min**, and in **55min** come to *the* tunnel — not for the claustrophobic! The path is good; the tunnel wide and tall, but it will take *at least 30 minutes to pass.* **Each member of the party must have a good torch.**

Exit from the tunnel at a large basin and then cross a spillway to join the levada path. Soon reach the first scree area (a second will be met 10 minutes later). **If the scree is not shored up the walk must be abandoned now.** Waterflow, storms and goats cause landslides at any time, and the damage will not be put right until the levada builders need to use the path to make repairs. The name 'Cascalho', by the way, conjures up visions of cascading waterfalls: but the name really means gravel or *scree!* If you can pass, you should find railings (again, turn back if these have come down) protecting the last bit of the way into the bowl of

The magnificent falls at Cascalho stream into a semi-circular basin from Bica da Cana on the Paúl da Serra, some 600 metres above

Cascalho, reached in **1h50min.** The photograph above can hardly do the setting justice, for we haven't a fish-eye lens!

Count yourself lucky if you reach your destination before mists fall! In our experience they fall very rapidly, usually by noon. Take any photographs *immediately*, before lunch. One of the best picnic spots is the far western side of the bowl, just before the levada narrows and disappears round a bend, where the walking is for mountain goats only!*

If your return walk is misty, the sheer drops to the right will be hidden from view; you will have time to notice here and there another indigenous Madeiran laurel — the white-barked *pau branco*. Its gnarled and grotesque arms provide your only contact with 'reality', as you walk along almost literally suspended in clouds. . . .

*And for levada-workers, of course. In the late 1980s, work is going on at this western side of the 'bowl'. They are tunnelling into the rock to tap a greater water supply for the Rabaças levada. Hopefully this will not affect the walk. Check the STOP PRESS.

The Ginjas waterhouse, below, is one of many delightful cottages where the levada workers keep their tools. Many have lovingly-tended gardens, full of flowers, and bordered by neatly-manicured hedges (Walks 20, 23)

23 ENCUMEADA · PINÁCULO · CARAMUJO · GINJAS WATERHOUSE · FEITEIRAS (OR ENCUMEADA)

See STOP PRESS   MAP is on reverse of touring map

Distance: 19km/11¾mi; 7h (or 15km/9¼mi; 6h back to Encumeada)

Grade: very strenuous; steep ascent and descent; only recommended in dry conditions

Equipment: walking boots, long trousers, whistle, sunhat, cardigans, anorak, picnic, plastic bottle with purifying tablets; torch if returning to Encumeada via the tunnels

How to get there: 🚐 6 to Encumeada
Depart Funchal 07.30; arrive Encumeada 09.40
To return: 🚐 6: Depart Feiteiras 15.15; depart Encumeada 15.45; arrive Funchal 17.45

Short walk: Go as far as energy permits along the route of the main walk: only stout shoes, sunhat, picnic and water are required. This short walk may be combined with those suggested under Walks 20, 21 and 22, to make a day out at Encumeada. 🚐 6 passes at 15.45

Photo references: see opposite and pages 26, 28, 100, 104. In our picture book, *Madeira* (1987 edition), see pages 50—51, 57, 70—71, 107, 118, 122—123, 124—125, 126, 128—129

An alternative to Walk 20, and an altogether more rewarding excursion for the energetic. You'll see *far* more on this walk — the landscapes are more varied, and you do not *have* to go through any tunnels! But the price to be paid is a climb of 500m/1650ft up to the 'Pinnacle' and a descent of 1300m/4265ft into Feiteiras. And you'll not be able to make the No 6 bus connection at Feiteiras unless you're lucky enough to be offered a lift along the EN208, which you meet just above Caramujo. To be *assured* of catching the No 6 bus, take a torch with you and return to *Encumeada*, via the tunnels (1h30min; see notes for Walk 20).

Leave the bus at Encumeada and continue north up the main road over the crest of the pass, to the viewpoint and picnicking area. Roadworks are in progress here: the EN204 is climbing to meet its westerly arm on the Paúl da Serra. While the great earthmovers roar away, the first part of this walk will not be very pleasant for some time to come*.

Start out by heading up the new road. You will find yourself climbing above and parallel to the Norte and Rabaças

*As this third edition goes to press, it is unclear how much the new road will change the first part of this walk. It appears that the first hour's walking (to the turn-off up to the Levada do Lombo do Mouro) will be along the new road, and you are likely to meet roadworks. Don't give up immediately! The road-builders have made every effort to keep this walk open, cutting new paths when necessary. Simply say 'Pee-**nah**-koo-loh', and, if they have cut a new route off the roadworks, they will point you in the right direction.

levadas (Walks 20–22), and you will have a bird's-eye view of their sinuous meanderings during the first part of the walk. All round, the mountains are clothed in the giant heath trees that give them their characteristic 'velvety' appearance.

When the road goes into a tunnel entrance (at **10min**), turn down left to an old narrow footpath. In **1h** you will be above the giant waterfall on the Rabaças levada. Soon

High in the clouds! From the fern- and flower-bright Levada da Serra, you'll look out east to the moorlands beyond Pico do Arieiro. The views from here, up on the eastern slopes of the Paúl da Serra, are magnificent; see also photograph page 111

approach a steep flight of stone steps. Turn up *sharp right* just *before* these steps, to follow a clear path to the Levada do Lombo do Mouro. There is another giant waterfall here, where you can collect water.

Turning right on the Levada do Lombo do Mouro, follow it until it ends, from where another clear path leads up ... and up ... and up to the Levada da Serra (**1h50min**). Relax now — and enjoy some good and easy walking along a grassy path, with magnificent views over the north coast and the valley leading to São Vicente. You'll soon see Pináculo rising up ahead to the right and meet the giant basalt pinnacle in **2h15min** walking. Just past Pináculo is our favourite lunch spot: here you may sit in long golden grasses beneath waterfalls surging and foaming over a huge and mossy basalt rock face. The soft valley of the Ribeira Sêca lies before you, leading down to São Vicente and the chapel of Nossa Senhora da Fâtima. Hawks circle watchfully above, and in summertime the grasses are ablaze with foxgloves and butterflies.

Following along the levada, come in **2h25min** to a grassy verge, where a path leads up left to Bica da Cana and a sign points straight on to Caramujo. In **2h30min** the levada's source is met; continue ahead along the path — waist deep in lime-green ferns in summer. All along here, the views over Rosário and to the great peaks towering in the east are at their best. Before you've had time to notice it, the path changes character as it meanders to Caramujo: sometimes it's a stone trail, sometimes a riverbed, sometimes a grassy path. Giant heath tree bowers and broom 'trees' shade the way — and often obscure the path — as you near Caramujo. Everywhere singing springs and streams are pouring down to the right, to feed the Levada do Norte.

Keep a look-out for the old Caramujo houses, or you'll miss them! They are located near a cultivated field (the *only* sign of cultivation in this wilderness!). At **3h30min** the path disgorges onto the EN208, some 300m(yds) past an overgrown path off right to Caramujo. Turn right downhill. You'll cross the dry Levada do Inferno in **4h** and meet the Ginjas waterhouse at **4h30min**. From here it's 7.7km/4¾mi to the EN104 (**7h**) — or you can return to Encumeada by turning right onto the levada and going through the tunnels (reversing Walk 20; under **6h**) ... if you brought a torch!

Right: From the velvety spine of the Lombo do Mouro, the views of the great peaks are superb. The massive escarpment of Pico Grande is crowned by a 'knoll'. Beyond it, from right to left, find Arieiro, the spike of Pico do Gato, the jagged Torres, and finally Ruivo

24 ENCUMEADA · LEVADA DO LOMBO DO MOURO · RIBEIRA BRAVA

See STOP PRESS

Distance: 15km/9¼mi; 5h **MAP is on reverse of touring map**

Grade: strenuous, with a climb of 300m/985ft to start and a steep descent of 1300m/4265ft; **possibility of vertigo on the levada path**

Equipment/How to get there/Short walk: as Walk 23, page 108
To return: any eastbound bus from Ribeira Brava (4, 6, 7, 107)

Photo references: see below and pages 26, 28, 55, 100, 104, 109. In our picture book, *Madeira* (1987 edition), see pages 28−29, 50−51, 118, 122−123, 124−125, 126, 128, 129, 140

L andslides caused by the roadworks on the EN204 have prevented us from checking out this walk for the past two years. We include it in this new edition, however, because it is both spectacular and convenient for buses. See if you can do it: refer first to the **STOP PRESS** and *always be prepared to turn back!*

Use the notes for Walk 23 to **start out**. When you come to the steep flight of stone steps (just over **1h**), climb them and continue on the path until you come to the new road (**1h15min**). The road disappears into a tunnel at the right, but you go left for five minutes, until the road crosses the Levada do Lombo do Mouro. Here turn left down a path, to follow the fast-flowing water in its descent down the dragon-like spine of this *lombo* (the ridge separating two parallel ravines). The levada peters out above Apresentação (near where Walk 5 also ends). Your destination is in sight as you follow a cobbled track steeply downhill, to join a tarred road in Apresentação. Here turn left downhill to the EN101, coming into plane-shaded Ribeira Brava after **5h**.

25 A RAMBLE ROUND PRAZERES

Distance: 8.5km/5¼mi; 3h
Grade: very easy
Equipment: stout shoes, sunhat, picnic, water
How to get there: 🚌 107 to Prazeres
Depart Funchal 08.05; arrive Prazeres 11.30
To return: 🚌 107: Depart Prazeres 15.00; arrive Funchal 18.15
Short walk: Go to the coastal overlook (4km/2½mi *return*; under 1½h): stout shoes, sunhat, picnic, water
Photo references: see below and opposite, also page 32. In our picture book, *Madeira* (1987 edition), see pages 11, 24—25, 38—39

Prazeres — the pleasures. So well named. But this most enchanting market garden of the west is little known. Discover some of its pleasures for yourself, on a day trip. You may make a short ramble, or just laze with a picnic in poppy fields overlooking the sea.

Two faces of Prazeres: Overlook spectacular coastal terracing from Picnic 25a or (right) sun-drenched fields below the Paúl (Picnic 25b)

Start the ramble at the crossroads in Prazeres, by walking north up the EN210 for two minutes, to reach the Levada Calheta—Ponta do Pargo. Stroll east along its course for about three-quarters of an hour, under pine and eucalyptus, by ferny glens and lily banks. Up to the north, fair weather clouds create glorious patterns over the bracken-gold flanks of the Paúl da Serra. Lunch at a sunny promontory and then make your way back to the crossroads and into the village.

From the fountain, keep walking down right, past the vivid orchards and gardens of Prazeres. When the road ends in fields thick with poppies and thistles, you look straight down over the sea and the tiny hamlet of Jardim do Mar 550m/1800ft below east. To the west, fantastical cliffs hide the seaside village of Paúl do Mar from view.

Returning from your picnic spot to the village square and the main road, the panorama is equally spectacular: the massif of the Paúl da Serra rises, sombre and serene, above the sun-drenched delights of Prazeres.

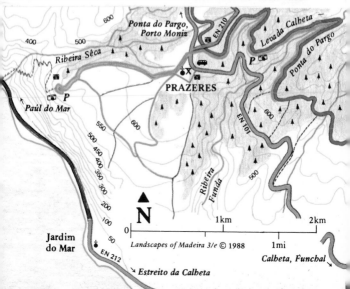

Landscapes of Madeira 3/e © 1988

Distance: 15km/9¼mi; 4¾h

MAP begins on page 120

Grade: quite easy, though often slippery — even overflowing! — on the Levada do Paúl; gradual descent to Rabaçal; some steep descents beyond Rabaçal and slight **possibility of vertigo** on the Levada Calheta—Ponta do Pargo

Equipment: stout shoes (boots in wet conditions), sunhat, anorak, cardigans, picnic, plastic bottle with water purifying tablets, whistle, torch

How to get there: 🚌 107 to Canhas *taxi rank*: departs Funchal 08.05; arrives 10.05. **NB:** the Canhas taxi rank is not in the village, but 1.5km/1mi west at Recta das Canhas *paragem* (pronounced '**Ray**-tah dahs **Cahn**-yahs'). As soon as you reach the village, look out for a statue representing the first station of the cross just by the church; just past the fourteenth station, see a large monument to St Theresa: leave the bus here; the taxi rank is on the opposite side of the road *Taxi from Canhas to Campo Grande*

To return: 🚌 107: depart Loreto 15.45; arrive Funchal 18.15

Short walks: Take equipment as above, including torch for no. 2

1 Walk as far as you like from Campo Grande along the Levada do Paúl; we would suggest as far as the caves (5km/3mi; 1½h *return*). Be sure to ask the taxi to wait for you. Wear stout shoes and a sunhat; take a picnic and water. Note that the path *may be very wet!*

2 Rabaçal to Loreto (7.5km/4¾mi; 3h). At Canhas, ask the taxi driver to take you to Rabaçal; start with notes on page 117, line 1. The walk is quite easy, but be prepared for some steep descents and slight **possibility of vertigo** on the Levada Calheta—Ponta do Pargo

Picture references: see below and pages 116—119. In our picture book, *Madeira* (1987 edition), see pages 42, 46, 86, 87, 90, 119

An awe-inspiring landscape, all stillness and solitude. The plateau of the Paúl da Serra stretches out before you, endlessly, under a porcelain-blue sky. Only your own shadow and a few sheep will walk with you on the 'marsh of the mountain range'.

At the Canhas taxi rank, ask for 'Cristo Rei' (**Crees**-toh **Ray**-ee) — Campo Grande'. The spot you want is 9km up the road from Canhas, just before a small statue of Christ the King. Here the road crosses the Levada do Paúl: there is a small white waterhouse on the right and four concrete markers on the left. This is one of the older levadas on Madeira, now integrated into the new scheme. Further east it is more aptly named the Levada da Bica da Cana, for it takes its source below Bica da Cana, in Ponta do Sol's river.

Begin the walk by striking out west, looking down over the moors to the lush south coast. The landscape is very reminiscent of the English Lake District or Derbyshire — yet with a difference: there is always the levada ribboning ahead of you — now silver, now amethyst, always mesmerising. There's a narrow path by a waterfall in about five minutes, but no further obstacles. The panorama stretching out before you seems to go on forever.

At **25min** pass a river pool, fed by a waterfall; reach a second in **45min**. Here, caves stretch up right into the hills.

'There is always the levada, ribboning ahead of you . . .' (Picnic 26a)

Animals — and sometimes shepherds — shelter here in bad weather. In April the hillside is crowned with golden gorse; the levada mirrors the sky; a few baby goats dare to gambol along your path. Cows graze freely on the lower slopes.

Now at **1h10min** an intrusion of the 20th century: you can see a metal conduit in the distance. It is carrying water from the reservoir above Rabaçal down to a power station. This *central*, commissioned in 1953, is unique on Madeira: its turbines feed on water from *three* levels of springs — see the map on pages 118–119. From the *central*, the water is sent in two levadas to irrigate the fields of Calheta (14km/ 8¾mi of channels) and Ponta do Pargo (40km/25mi).

At **1h15min** the Levada do Paúl flows into a mini-canal, well over 1m/3ft wide and just as deep! All is pouring into a reservoir, familiarly called 'the tank', before being funnelled down to the power station. There is an incredible feeling of *power* in the stillness.

Just behind the tank, take the road to Rabaçal, rounding a U-turn and crossing the Ribeira do Alecrim with its lovely pools at **1h25min**. Continue downhill under the watchful eyes of goats until at **1h40min** you arrive at Rabaçal. While this recently-renovated rest house is usually reserved for the use of government employees, an overnight stay can sometimes be arranged (see 'Where to stay', page 36).

Below: falls beyond the Rabaçal tunnel (Picnic 26d). Opposite: the Rabaçal houses (Picnic 26b) lie 200 metres below the reservoir (top left); company on the Levada das 25 Fontes (bottom left); and Risco's waterfall (Picnic 28) cascades into shimmering pools (right)

When the tarred road ends at Rabaçal, turn right down the dirt track. In **3min** come to the higher, Risco, levada (Walk 28). You will reach the fork to '25 Fontes' in 5min. Turn down left. Turn left again on reaching the levada. Fifteen minutes' walking along this enchanting, singing watercourse will bring you to a grassy sun-trap outside the entrance to the first major tunnel built on Madeira in the mid-1800s. Torrents of water cascade down sluices all round. It takes only ten minutes to pass this tunnel — the highest and widest on the island; soon you've left the shade of Rabaçal for the sunny heights of Calheta's *lombos*.

You'll find a keeper's cottage, a rustic picnic table and a tap. Continue left along the levada *until a small ravine has been crossed on the wooden bridge shown opposite.* Then follow the adjacent path down the valley through heath, mimosa and pine. In **2h40min** you will cross two pipes carrying water from the 'tank' down to the power station. Five minutes later, a single pipe holds the flow of the levadas of Risco and 25 Fontes. Soon meet the Levada da Rocha Vermelha and follow its course to a small tank, whence it too shoots down to the power station. From here, the way to the Levada Calheta—Ponta do Pargo is along a jeep track; you will reach the big levada in **3h15min**. Turn left and enjoy a sunny stroll with splendid views over the south coast. Some thirty-five minutes along the levada, turn right down any cobbled track to descend through scrumptious Florenças. Meet the main road at **4h15min**; turn left and find Loreto's plane-shaded square and chapel after **4h45min**.

The photographs:
To the left are views of the tunnel exit at Rabaçal (just before Picnic 26d), part of the Risco falls (Picnic 28) and the mountains of Rabaçal (Picnic 26b). Opposite: looking north from the descent into Calheta's valley (Walk 26), the sun-trap below the Rabaçal houses, by sluices at the tunnel entrance (Picnic 26c), a view of the falls and pool at 25 Fontes (Walk 28)

N

Landscapes of Madeira © 1988

0   1km

½mi

Porto Moniz

EN204

Levada da Rocha

Levada Calheta

Ponta do Pargo

EN211

Atouguia

800
750
700
650
600

Ribeira da Calheta

Ribeira da

Ribeira das Faias

550

26
Florenças

500
450

Calheta

Ribeira da Atouguia

EN101

Loreto
400   ← Funchal

25 Fontes
950
28

Levada das 25 Fontes

Levada do Risco

900
1000
1100
1200
P
P ✗ Rabaçal
1100
1150
Risco
1200
1250
28
P
Risco
Ribeira Grande
1250
1300

Ribeira do Alecrim
EN204-1
1150
1200
1250

ermelha
1100
1200
26

1050
1000
950
900

Levada do Paúl
EN204
120
1100

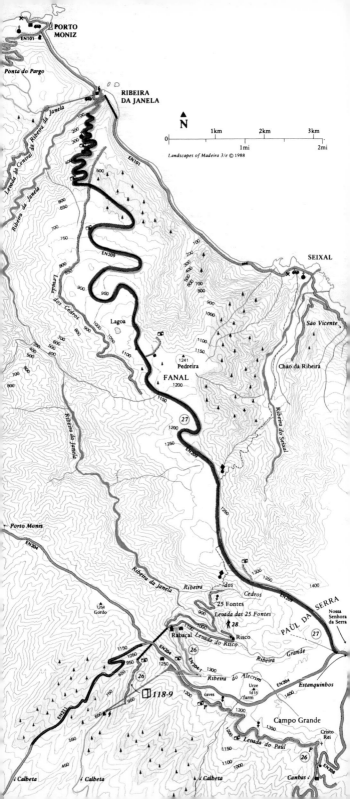

27 PAÚL DA SERRA · FANAL · RIBEIRA DA JANELA

Distance: 20.5km/12¾mi; 6½h   **MAP is on facing page**

Grade: easy for sturdy walkers and accessible even to beginners with lots of stamina; steep descent from the Fanal into Ribeira da Janela; recommended for summer months only; thick mists may descend!

Equipment: stout shoes (boots in wet conditions), sunhat, anorak, 2 cardigans, whistle, picnic, water

How to get there: 🚌 107 to Canhas *taxi rank* (see notes Walk 26!) Depart Funchal 08.05; arrive Canhas 10.05
Taxi from Canhas: ask for 'Nossa Senhora da Serra' (see page 122)
To return from Canhas: 🚌 107: depart 16.15; arrive Funchal 18.15
To return from Ribeira da Janela: 🚌 150 to São Vicente: depart Ribeira da Janela 14.20, to connect with 🚌 6 (it will wait for the No 150); arrive Funchal 17.45

Short walk: Paúl da Serra to the Rabaçal/north coast overlook (3km/ under 2mi; 1h *return*); stout shoes, sunhat, picnic, water

Alternative walk: Paúl da Serra to the Fanal and return (about 14km/ 8¾mi; 4½h *return*). This walk allows you to see much of the best of the long walk and still catch the afternoon bus from Canhas: but you'll have to walk quickly if you want to picnic as well! Ask the taxi driver to wait for you or return for you — whichever is cheaper!

Photo references: see pages 31, 114—115, 117 and 118. In our picture book, *Madeira* (1987 edition), see pages 8, 10, 14—15, 23, 98—99, 102—103, 116—117

T he air will be crystal-clear, the panorama endless; and even with the sun fully up, dew-drops will sparkle on the gold-green grasses of the Paúl. At present, this is the 'perfect' long walk on Madeira, for it's within the reach of everyone with stamina. And, at present, your only companions will be sea gulls, cows and goats — and blue and yellow butterflies riding on your shoulder.

Indeed, this walk is such a joy that we have included it in this updated edition of *Landscapes*, even though it does have two drawbacks: it is not easily accessible by public transport and roadworks have obliterated the original trail.

You cannot make the walk as we describe it and return to Funchal the same day by bus, unless the timetables are changed. Several alternatives present themselves, the most obvious being to share a hire car with someone touring the west of the island, who can collect you at Ribeira da Janela. An overnight stay at Vinháticos or the new hotel at Ribeira Brava will bring you closer to the walk — but you will still need an early morning taxi. You can start the walk later in the day if you plan to go on to Porto Moniz for the night — see **STOP PRESS**.

Finally, the Alternative walk described above is a good possibility. It allows you to see much of the best of the long walk — the Fanal and the north coast views; it's less strenuous than the long walk, and bus connections are better. Be sure to arrange with the Canhas taxi driver to *collect you* from the starting point, in time for the return bus.

The new road is a more serious drawback, because you may find roadworks in progress, with all the attendant roar and disruption. But every cloud has a silver lining: in the past, it was possible in heavy mists to get lost on the old trail across the Paúl, but not any longer! At present the road bed is already cut, and you can follow the route easily. And in future, even if the road is metalled, it is doubtful that it will bear much traffic. Only time will tell whether we have really lost one of the island's most enchanting walks.

The walk starts on the Paúl da Serra, 13km/8mi north of Canhas, just before a statue (Nossa Senhora da Serra). Here there is a sign 'Fanal 8km/Ribeira da Janela 10km'. The first indication is correct, but Ribeira da Janela is *20.5km/ 12¾mi* from here! Look forward northwest to see two ranges of afforested hills: the new road runs between them. You may notice, too, the stone wall which separates the Paúl proper from Campo Grande, starting point for Walk 26. Look over left to see the channel from the northern branch of the Levada do Paúl snaking its way towards the 'tank' (Walk 26), and the outline of the EN204 to Porto Moniz. But up ahead is only endless landscape, shimmering.

By **25min** into the walk you reach the very deep valley of the Ribeira dos Cedros on the left and the track bends to the right. Five minutes later, you'll be able to overlook the red-tiled roofs of the Rabaçal houses, and just above them, the edge of the reservoir. Anywhere here, where you can see the north coast or the mountains surrounding Rabaçal, is a delightful place to finish the short walk with a picnic.

At **1h05min** follow a short path to the right for some excellent views of the valley of the Ribeira do Seixal. By **1h30min** you reach the spot where an old path descends to the Levada das 25 Fontes and thence to Rabaçal (beyond the sage-green clearing on the left). And then at **1h45min** you'll pass the old path down to Seixal via Chão da Ribeira. *(Both of these paths are overgrown and hazardous. They should only be attempted by expert mountain walkers in the company of a guide, in high summer.)*

Soon (**1h50min**) you approach a crest. Walk to the right of the roadworks and see the waves crashing in on the north coast. Look ahead to see a dew-pond area swirling with sea-gulls. Behind it is a cone-shaped mound with trees parading up its left flank — Pedreira — landmark of the Fanal. Wisely, the road skirts the Fanal. The old trail has been closed off (this is for the protection of the area). Come to a track off right to a forestry house, and make for the parkland (**2h 05min**). Fences of dried heath trees keep the cows and goats from wandering. This is a wonderland of ancient trees, gnarled into whimsical shapes, deep grey-green against the golden grass and bracken, turned to russet in September. When you're well to the back of Pedreira, climb up the promontory at the right for lunch. Here you look down on the breathtaking beauty of Chão da Ribeira and the sea.

Reluctantly leaving the Fanal, you become ever more aware of the very deep valley opening up on your left, the ravine of Madeira's largest river. Reach and cross the Levada dos Cedros in about **3h40min**, and soon have magnificent views of your destination, and behind it, the terraces of Porto Moniz. Between the two villages catch the outline of the 16km/10mi long Levada da Central da Ribeira da Janela carrying water from tributaries of the great river down to the power station (1965).

Soon you see the first *palheiros* on the outskirts of the village. Grapes are growing on trellises over the crops here, as elsewhere; this not only brings two simultaneous harvests from the land, but the grape leaves are used as fertiliser.

By about **4h50min** you'll reach the first houses. It's a *very* steep descent if you take the cobbled steps leading down to the church and then to the main road far below. We would advise you to stay on the roadworks all the way down; we've allowed over 90 minutes for the descent to the power station where you catch the 150 bus.

Russet bracken and giant til trees give the Fanal its unique flavour

NB: A tunnel (to tap additional water for the Risco levada) is being built at the Risco falls in the late 1980s, and the levada-workers' track has temporarily destroyed the old mossy way. We are certain that it will regain its former beauty, so we have not altered our description. While work is in progress, the walk to 25 Fontes may be impassable, as debris from the higher (Risco) levada causes landslides

Distance: 7km/4¼mi; 2½h   **MAP is on page 119**

Grade: very easy to Risco; the walk to 25 Fontes is along a level, but **vertiginous and unprotected** path — only for experts!

Equipment: walking boots, cardigans, long trousers, sunhat, anorak, whistle, rainhat, picnic, plastic bottle with water purifying tablets

How to get there: 🚌 107 to Canhas *taxi rank* (see notes **Walk 26!**) *Canhas taxi to and from Rabaçal* (or walk to Loreto; see page 117) *To return:* 🚌 107: Depart Canhas 16.15; arrive Funchal 18.15

Short walks: No special equipment is required for either — just good shoes, cardigans and a picnic

1   Rabaçal to Risco: 30min *return*, signposted (see above!)

2   Rabaçal to the waterhouse on the Levada das 25 Fontes: 50min *return*; the path is not vertiginous before the waterhouse

Photo references: see pages 116—119. In our picture book, *Madeira* (1987 edition), see pages 86, 87, 90

R abaçal is an enchanted fairyland of singing waterfalls, and a favourite excursion spot amongst the Madeirans. Here at the head of Madeira's greatest valley, the Rabaçal houses lie dwarfed beneath emerald-cloaked mountains.

The walk begins just where the road ends at Rabaçal. Turn right down the dirt track. In three minutes you reach the higher (Risco) levada. The banks are built up high to cope with the even greater flow of water the new source will provide. When you reach the fork (to 25 Fontes) in **5min**, stay on the higher levada and in **9min** ford the spill-way created by a waterfall on the right. Here the levada is flanked by an exceedingly beautiful mossy 'carpet'. You reach Risco in **13min**. Here two falls cascade into a pool 35m/115ft deep, from a height of 100m/325ft. A tunnel is being built just below the concrete channel which encircles the falls. If no work is in progress, this is an excellent lunch spot, and you can chill your *vinho verde* in the levada! From here you can see the levada continue around the head of the gorge and along the valley opposite to its source in the Ribeira Grande. Look below — across the valley — to see a second channel cut into the mountainside: this is the lower levada, leading to 25 Fontes.

If you don't mind getting soaking wet, you can go as far as the lookout under the waterfall to see Risco's pool, but *go no further!* The levada is completely crumbled away.

Now retrace your steps back to the fork (**21min**). Climb

down stone steps to reach the Levada das 25 Fontes. Turn right and in **30min** you will see the Risco waterfalls again, from a lower level. The views are not quite as good, but if you're pressed for time (or if levada works preclude a visit to Risco — see NB above), you could follow this levada only and still glimpse Risco's falls: in **40min** you come to the head of the gorge where they dive down. Then cross the bed of the Ribeira Grande, to meet a tiny waterhouse.

After this point, those who suffer from vertigo should *turn back*. The ledge is only 30cm/1ft wide in places, and there are no railings to protect you from the drops at the left — some up to 30m/100ft. But this levada is a bit different from others. It is built *up* off the path, not sunk into it. Here the concrete edge of the levada is at waist level (see photo page 117), and you can hold on to the levada channel if the drops worry you. It's lovely to run your hands in the water or cool yourself on a hot day.

In about **1h10min** walking, you reach a path leading up right (by a sluice) and at once you see a semi-circular bowl into which tumble down many sparkling waterfalls. It's a lovely place to paddle under ferns on a hot day. But, alas, as Madeirans will be quick to tell you, this spot is not as beautiful as it was when they were young! Most of the springs have been diverted from the '25 Waterfalls' to the levada and from there to the fields in the southwest.

BUS TIMETABLES

Below is a list of destinations covered by the following seven pages of timetables. Numbers following the place names are *bus numbers*; they are arranged in numerical order. See page 9 for more bus information; see also pages 10-11 for bus departure points.

Arco de São Jorge 103
Assomada 2 (& as Machico)
*Babosas 22 (see also Monte)
Boaventura 6, 103
Boa Morte 148
Boqueirão 60
*Botanical Gardens 30
Cabo Girão 154
Camacha 29, 77
Câmara de Lobos 1, 4, 6, 7, 96, 107, 154
Campanário 4, 6, 7, 107
Canhas 107
Caniçal 113
Caniço 2, 23, 25, 53, 78, 113, 136, 155
Corticeiras 96
Cruzinhas 103

Curral das Freiras 81
Encumeada 6
Estreito de Câmara de Lobos 4, 6, 7, 96, 107, 154
Faial 53, 78, 103
Gaula 60
Lombo Grande 60
Machico 20, 23, 53, 78, 113
Madalena do Mar 4
*Monte 20, 21, 103
Palheiro Ferreiro 29, 30, 77
Poiso 103
Ponta da Oliveira 155
Ponta Delgada 6
Ponta do Pargo 107, 150
Ponta do Sol 4, 107
Ponte dos Frades 1
Portela 53

Porto da Cruz 53, 78
Porto Moniz 150
Raposeira 107
Ribeira Brava 4, 6, 7, 107
Ribeira Sêca 113
Ribeira da Janela 150
Ribeiro Frio 103
Rosário 6
Santa 150
Santa Cruz 9, 23, 25, 113
Santana 103
Santo Amaro 42
Santo da Serra 20, 25, 77, 78
São Jorge 103
São Vicente 6, 150
Seixal 150
Serra de Água 6
Vinháticos 6

*Departures for **Monte, Babosas, Botanical Gardens** too frequent to list

BUS 2
Funchal—
Assomada

Funchal	Assomada	Assomada	Funchal
departs	arrives	departs	arrives
	Mondays to Saturdays		
07.30	08.10	06.20	07.00
08.30	09.10	07.10	07.50
10.00	10.40	07.45	08.25
11.00	11.40	08.15	08.55
11.45	12.25	09.30	10.10
12.45	13.25	11.00	11.40
14.00	14.40	11.40	12.20
15.00	15.40	12.35	13.15
16.00	16.40	13.45	14.25
17.00	17.40	14.45	15.25
17.30	18.10	16.00	16.40
18.45	19.25	17.00	17.40
19.30	20.10	17.45	18.25
20.15	20.55	18.30	19.10
21.00	21.40	19.30	20.10
22.45	23.25	22.00	22.40
00.15	00.55	23.30	24.10
	Sundays and holidays		
07.30	08.10	06.45	07.25
08.30	09.10	08.30	09.10
10.00	10.40	09.30	10.10
11.00	11.40	11.00	11.40
12.00	12.40	12.00	12.40
13.00	13.40	13.30	14.10
15.00	15.40	15.00	15.40
16.30	17.10	17.00	17.40
18.00	18.40	18.00	18.40
19.00	19.40	19.00	19.40
20.30	21.20	22.00	22.40
22.45	23.25	23.30	00.10
00.15	00.55		

BUS 4
Funchal—
Ribeira
Brava—
Ponta do
Sol; the
10.00 bus
goes on to
Madalena
do Mar;
both return
buses start
at Madalena

Funchal	Estreito de C de Lobos	Campanário	Ribeira Brava	Ponta do Sol
	Mondays to Saturdays			
10.05	10.35	11.05	11.25	12.00
	Mondays to Fridays			
14.05	14.35	15.05	15.25	16.00

Ponta do Sol	Ribeira Brava	Campanário	Estreito de C de Lobos	Funchal
	Daily except Sundays and 25 December			
12.55	13.30	13.50	14.25	14.55
	Sundays only (but not 25 December)			
11.45	12.20	12.40	13.15	13.45

BUS 6
Funchal—
Ribeira
Brava—
Encumeada
—São
Vicente—
Boaventura

Funchal	Câmara de Lobos	Campanário	Ribeira Brava	Serra de Água
07.35*	07.50*	08.35*	08.55*	09.20*
13.35**	13.50**	14.35**	14.55**	15.20**
17.05***	17.20***	18.00***	18.20***	18.45***

Encumeada	Rosário	São Vicente	Pta Delgada	Boaventura
09.40*	10.00*	10.15*	10.35*	10.45*
15.40**	16.00**	16.15**	16.35**	16.45**
19.10***	19.30*	19.45***	20.05***	20.15***

Boaventura	Pta Delgada	São Vicente	Rosário	Encumeada
05.50****	06.00****	06.20****	06.35****	06.55****
07.00***	07.10***	07.30***	07.45***	08.05***
14.40*	14.50*	15.10*	15.25*	15.45*

Serra de Água	Ribeira Brava	Campanário	Câmara de Lobos	Funchal
07.15****	07.40****	07.55****	08.30****	08.45****
08.25***	08.50***	09.05***	09.40***	09.55***
16.05*	16.30*	16.50*	17.30*	17.45*

*   Daily except December 25
**   Mondays to Saturdays
***   Daily except Good Friday and December 25, 26, 31
****   Mondays to Saturdays, except for first Saturday in September

BUS 7
Funchal—
Ribeira
Brava

Funchal	Estreito de C de Lobos	Campanário	Ribeira Brava
Mondays to Fridays			
06.45	07.35	08.00	08.15
09.30	10.20	10.45	11.00
10.50	11.40	12.05	12.20
14.05	14.55	15.20	15.35
15.35	16.25	16.50	17.05
17.05	17.55	18.20	18.35
18.35*	19.25*	19.50*	20.05*
20.15	21.05	21.30	21.45
Saturdays, Sundays and holidays			
06.45**	07.35**	08.00**	08.15**
10.05***	10.55***	11.20***	11.35***
10.50**	11.40**	12.05**	12.20**
12.05***	12.55***	13.20***	13.35***
13.35	14.25	14.50	15.05
15.35	16.25	16.50	17.05
17.05	17.55	18.20	18.35
20.15	21.05	21.30	21.45

Ribeira Brava	Campanário	Estreito de C de Lobos	Funchal
Mondays to Fridays			
06.05	06.20	06.45	07.35
08.15	08.30	08.55	09.45
11.00	11.15	11.40	12.30
12.35	12.50	13.15	14.05
15.30	15.45	16.10	17.00
17.05	17.20	17.45	18.35
18.35	18.50	19.15	20.05
Saturdays, Sundays and holidays			
06.05**	06.20**	06.45**	07.35**
08.15**	08.30**	08.55**	09.45**
11.00**	11.15**	11.40**	12.30**
11.45***	12.00***	12.25***	13.15***
12.30**	12.45**	13.10**	14.00**
13.35***	13.50***	14.15***	15.00***
15.30	15.45	16.10	17.00
17.05	17.20	17.45	18.35
18.35	18.50	19.15	20.05

*   Not on 31 December or 1 January
**   Only on Saturdays
***   Only on Sundays
No buses on Christmas Day

BUS 20
**Funchal—
Santa Cruz
— Machico
— Santo
da Serra**

Funchal	Santa Cruz	Machico	Santo da Serra
07.15*	08.05*	08.15*	09.05*
12.30*	13.20*	13.30*	14.20*
12.45**	13.35**	13.45**	14.35**
16.30*	17.20*	17.30*	18.20*
19.15***	20.05***	20.15***	21.05***

Santo da Serra	Machico	Santa Cruz	Funchal
06.30*	07.20*	07.30*	08.20*
08.00*	08.50*	09.00*	09.50*
09.30*	10.20*	10.30*	11.20*
14.30***	15.20***	15.30***	16.20***

* Not on Sundays or holidays
** Only on Sundays
*** Not on Saturdays, Sundays or holidays

BUS 23
**Funchal—
Santa Cruz
—Machico**

Funchal	Machico	Machico	Funchal
departs	arrives	departs	arrives
06.45*	07.45*	05.30*	06.30*
08.00*	09.00*	06.30*	07.30*
09.00**	10.00**	07.30*	08.30*
10.30	11.30	08.30	09.30
11.30**	12.30**	09.30*	10.30*
11.45*	12.45*	11.30**	12.30**
13.30**	14.30**	11.45*	12.45*
15.00**	16.00**	12.30**	13.30**
15.45**	16.45*	12.45*	13.45*
16.00*	17.00*	13.15**	14.15*
17.45*	18.45*	16.00**	17.00**
18.00**	19.00**	17.30**	18.30*
19.00**	20.00**	18.30**	19.30**
20.00**	21.00**	20.15**	21.15**
21.00**	22.00**	22.30***	23.30***
21.30***	22.30***		

BUS 25
*see top of
next page*

* Only on Sundays and holidays
** Not on Sundays and holidays
*** Not on Saturdays, Sundays or holidays

BUS 29
**Funchal—
Palheiro
Ferreiro
—Camacha**

Funchal	Camacha	Camacha	Funchal
departs	arrives	departs	arrives
	Mondays to Saturdays		
08.00	08.40	07.00	07.40
09.00	09.40	07.15*	07.55*
10.00	10.40	07.45*	08.25*
11.00	11.40	08.15	08.55
11.45	12.25	08.45	09.25
13.00*	13.40*	09.45	10.25
13.30	14.10	10.45	11.25
14.45*	15.25*	11.45	12.25
15.30	16.10	12.30	13.10
16.30*	17.10*	13.45*	14.25*
17.00*	17.40*	14.15	14.55
17.30	18.10	15.30*	16.10*
18.00*	18.40*	16.15	16.55
18.30*	19.10*	17.15*	17.55*
19.00	19.40	17.45*	18.25*
19.30*	20.10*	18.15	18.55
20.00*	20.40*	18.45*	19.25*
20.30	21.10	19.15*	19.55*
22.00*	22.40*	19.45	20.25
23.30*	00.10*	22.45*	23.30*
	Sundays and holidays		
09.15	09.55	08.30	09.10
10.00	10.40	10.00	10.40
11.00	11.40	11.00	11.40
12.30	13.10	11.45	12.25
15.30	16.10	14.45	15.25
17.00	17.40	16.15	16.55
19.00	19.40	17.45	18.25
20.45	21.10	20.15	20.45

(column note, Funchal–Camacha side): passes Palheiro Ferreiro 25 minutes later

(column note, Camacha–Funchal side): passes Palheiro Ferreiro 20 minutes later

* Not on Saturdays   No buses 25 December

BUS 25
Funchal—
Santo da
Serra

Funchal	Santo da Serra	Santo da Serra	Funchal
	Sundays only		
08.45	10.05	16.15*	17.35*
		17.45**	19.05**

* Only from 1/10 to 31/5
** Only from 1/6 to 30/9

BUS 53
Funchal—
Portela—
Porto da
Cruz—Faial

Funchal	Portela	Porto da Cruz	Faial
Mondays to Saturdays (except holidays)			
10.00	11.50	12.10	12.30
13.00	14.50	15.10	15.30
17.15*	19.05	19.25	19.45
19.15*	21.05*	21.25*	21.45*
Sundays and holidays (except 25 December)			
18.15	20.05	20.25	20.45

Faial	Porto da Cruz	Portela	Funchal
Mondays to Saturdays			
15.00	15.20	15.40	17.30
16.30	16.50	17.10	19.00
Daily (except 25 December)			
10.00	10.20	10.40	12.30

* Not on Saturdays

BUS 60
Funchal—
Gaula—
Boqueirão

Funchal		Boqueirão	Boqueirão		Funchal
11.00	*passes Gaula 45min later*	12.15	07.30*	*passes Gaula 30min later*	08.45*
14.00*		15.15*	08.30*		09.45*
17.00*		18.15*	12.30**		13.45**
17.30**		18.45*	16.00**		17.15**
19.15*		20.30*	16.30*		17.45*

* Not on Sundays or holidays
** Only on Sundays and holidays

BUS 77
Funchal—
Santo da
Serra

Funchal	Palheiro Ferreiro	Camacha	Santo da Serra
08.30**	08.55**	09.10**	09.50**
10.30***	10.55***	11.10***	11.50***
14.00	14.25	14.40	15.20
18.00***	18.25***	18.40***	19.20***
19.15*	19.40*	19.55*	20.35*

Santo da Serra	Camacha	Palheiro Ferreiro	Funchal
06.30****	07.10****	07.25****	07.50****
07.15	07.50	08.05	08.30
12.00*	12.40*	12.55*	13.20*
16.15**	16.55**	17.10**	17.35**
18.00**	18.40**	18.55**	19.15**
20.40****	21.20****	21.35****	21.55****

*   only from 1.4 to 30.9
**   Only on Sundays and holidays
***   Not on Sundays and holidays
**** Not on Saturdays, Sundays or holidays
No buses 25 December

BUS 78
Funchal—
Portela—
Faial

Funchal	Faial	Faial	Funchal
08.00***	10.45***	06.30*	09.15*
12.30**	15.15**	07.00**	09.45**
16.15*	19.00**	17.30***	20.15***

*   Not on Sundays or holidays
**   Only on holidays
*** Only on Sundays
No buses 25 December. Buses pass Portela and Porto da Cruz. See approximate times under Bus 53

BUS 81
Funchal—
Curral das
Freiras

Funchal		Curral das Freiras		Funchal
departs	arrives	departs		arrives
05.45*	07.00*	05.45****		07.00****
09.15**	10.30**	06.45*		08.00*
11.00*	12.15*	11.00**		12.15**
13.15***	14.30***	12.15*		13.30*
16.30	17.45	14.30***		15.45***
18.45*****	20.00*****	17.45		19.00
		19.45*****		21.00*****

*	Not on Sundays or holidays
**	Only on Sundays and holidays (except 25 December)
***	Not on Saturdays, Sundays or holidays
****	Only Mondays
*****	Only Fridays

BUS 96
Funchal—
Corticeiras

Funchal	Ponte dos Frades	Estreito de C de Lobos	Corticeiras
Mondays to Fridays			
07.00	07.35	07.45	08.00
08.05	08.40	08.50	09.05
09.00	09.35	09.45	10.00
09.45	10.20	10.30	10.45
10.45	11.20	11.30	11.45
11.45	12.20	12.30	12.45
12.15	12.50	13.00	13.15
13.15	13.50	14.00	14.15
15.15	15.50	16.00	16.15
16.15	16.50	17.00	17.15
16.45	17.20	17.30	17.45
17.35	18.10	18.20	18.35
18.15	18.50	19.00	19.15
18.45	19.20	19.30	19.45
19.15	19.50	20.00	20.15
Saturdays, Sundays and holidays (except 25 December)			
07.00	07.40	07.50	08.05
08.00	08.40	08.50	09.05
09.15	09.50	10.00	10.15
11.15	11.40	11.50	12.15
13.00	13.40	13.50	14.05
15.00	15.40	15.50	16.05
16.00	16.40	16.50	17.05
17.30	18.10	18.20	18.35
18.45	19.20	19.30	19.45
19.45	20.20	20.30	20.45

Corticeiras	Estreito de C de Lobos	Ponte dos Frades	Funchal
Mondays to Fridays			
06.00	06.15	06.25	07.00
06.45	07.00	07.10	07.45
08.05	08.20	08.30	09.05
09.05	09.20	09.30	10.05
10.15	10.30	10.40	11.15
11.00	11.15	11.25	12.00
12.00	12.15	12.25	13.00
12.45	13.00	13.40	13.45
13.15	13.30	13.40	14.15
14.15	14.30	14.40	15.15
16.15	16.30	16.40	17.15
17.15	17.30	17.40	18.15
17.45	18.00	18.10	18.45
19.45	20.00	20.10	20.45
Saturdays, Sundays and holidays (except 25 December)			
05.45	06.00	06.10	06.45
08.00	08.25	08.35	09.10
09.00	09.20	09.30	10.05
10.15	10.30	10.40	11.15
11.00	11.15	11.25	12.00
12.15	13.00	13.10	13.45
14.00	14.20	14.30	15.05
16.00	16.20	16.30	17.05
17.00	17.20	17.30	18.05
18.30	18.50	19.00	19.35

BUS 103
Funchal—
Poiso—
Santana—
Boaventura

Funchal	Monte	Poiso	Cruzinhas	Faial
07.00	07.25	08.00	08.30	08.45
13.30*	13.55*	14.30*	15.00*	15.15*
16.00*	16.25*	17.00*	17.30*	17.45*
18.00**	18.25**	19.00**	19.30**	19.45**

Santana	São Jorge	Arco de São Jorge		Boaventura
09.15	09.45	10.15		10.45
15.45*	16.15*	16.45*		17.15*
18.15*	18.45*	19.15*		19.45*
20.15**	20.45**	21.15**		21.45**

Boaventura	Arco de São Jorge		São Jorge	Santana
05.30*	06.00*		06.30*	07.00*
07.15	07.45		08.15	08.45
12.00*	12.30*		13.00*	13.30*
16.00	16.30		17.00	17.30

Faial	Cruzinhas	Poiso	Monte	Funchal
07.30*	07.45*	08.15*	08.35*	09.00*
09.15	09.30	10.00	10.25	11.00
14.00*	14.15*	14.45*	15.10*	15.45*
18.00	18.15	18.45	19.10	19.45

* Not on Sundays, January 1, Good Friday, August 15, December 25 or 26
** Not on August 14 or December 25

BUS 107
Funchal—
Ribeira
Brava—
Canhas—
Raposeira—
Ponta do
Pargo

Funchal	Câmara de Lobos	Ribeira Brava	Canhas	Raposeira*
The bus below runs daily except for December 25th				
08.05	08.20	09.30	10.05	11.45
The bus below does not run on Sundays, January 1, January 6, December 25, December 26, December 31				
16.05	16.20	17.30	18.15	19.45

Raposeira*	Canhas	Ribeira Brava	Câmara de Lobos	Funchal
The bus below does not run on Sundays, Mondays, January 1, January 6, December 25, December 26, December 31				
06.30	08.00	08.45	09.45	10.00
The bus below runs daily except for December 25th				
14.45	16.15	17.00	18.00	18.15

* The bus arriving Raposeira at 11.45 departs for Ponta do **Pargo** at 13.00, after a lunch break. The bus arriving Raposeira at 19.45 terminates there. The bus departing Raposeira 06.30 starts out there; the bus departing at 14.45 starts out from Ponta do **Pargo** at 13.45

BUSES 113,
150, 154

see next page

see next page

BUS 155
Funchal—
Ponta da
Oliveira

Funchal	Pta da Oliveira	Pta da Oliveira	Funchal
departs	*arrives*	*departs*	*arrives*
Mondays to Saturdays			
06.30*	07.10	07.15*	07.55
08.20**	09.00	09.00**	09.40
10.15*	10.55	11.00*	11.40
13.30**	14.10	14.15**	14.55
14.15*	14.55	15.00*	15.40
17.15**	17.55	18.15**	18.55
19.15*	19.55	20.00*	20.40
Sundays and holidays			
13.30**	14.10	09.00**	09.40
17.15**	17.55	14.15**	14.55
		18.15**	18.55

* via Garajau
** via Figueirinhas
No buses on 25 December

BUS 113
Funchal—
Machico—
Caniçal

Funchal	Santa Cruz	Machico	Caniçal
07.30	08.20	08.35	09.10
09.00	09.50	10.05	10.40
11.15	12.05	12.20	12.55
12.00**	12.50**	13.05**	13.40**
12.15	13.05	13.20	13.55
14.30	15.20	15.35	16.10
15.30	16.20	16.35	17.10
16.30**	17.20**	17.35**	18.10**
17.15	18.05	18.25	18.55

Caniçal	Machico	Santa Cruz	Funchal
05.45***	06.10***	06.30***	07.20***
06.30	07.00	07.20	08.10
09.30**	10.00**	10.20**	11.10**
10.15	10.45	11.05	11.55
11.30	12.00	12.20	13.10
13.00	13.30	13.50	14.40
14.00	14.30	14.50	15.40
17.00	17.30	17.50	18.40
18.00	18.30	18.50	19.40
19.00**	19.30**	19.50**	20.40**

Buses run daily except for 25 December and:
** Only on Sundays, January 1, January 6, Good Friday,
    Corpus Christi, June 10, August 15, November 1, December 8,
    December 26
*** Only on Mondays (except holidays)

BUS 148   *see page 58, 'Short walk 3'*

BUS 150
Ponta do
Pargo—
Porto
Moniz—
São
Vicente

Santa*	Porto Moniz	Ribeira da Janela	Seixal	São Vicente
06.30	06.45	06.50	07.10	07.30
14.00	14.15	14.20	14.40	14.55

São Vicente	Seixal	Ribeira da Janela	Porto Moniz	Santa*
10.25	10.40	11.00	11.05	11.20
16.30	16.50	17.10	17.15	17.30

* Bus departing Santa 06.30 originates there; bus departing Santa
14.00 starts out at 13.00 from **Ponta do Pargo**. The bus arriving
Santa at 11.20 goes on to **Ponta do Pargo** at 12.40, after a lunch
break; the bus arriving Santa 17.30 terminates there. *Buses run
daily except for Good Friday, December 25, 26, 31 and January 1*

BUS 154
Funchal—
Cabo Girão

Funchal	Ponte dos Frades	Estreito de C de Lobos	Cabo Girão
Mondays to Fridays			
09.15	09.50	10.05	10.15
14.35	15.10	15.25	15.35
Saturdays, Sundays and holidays (except for the first Sunday in September and 25 December)			
10.35	11.10	11.25	11.35

Cabo Girão	Estreito de C de Lobos	Ponte dos Frades	Funchal
Mondays to Fridays			
10.20	10.30	10.45	11.20
15.45	15.55	16.10	16.45
Saturdays, Sundays and holidays (except for the first Sunday in September and 25 December)			
11.50	12.00	12.15	12.50

BUS 155   *see foot of page 131*

Geographical entries only are included here; for other names, see Contents, page 3. All indexing is in Portuguese: eg Paradise Valley is indexed under 'Vale do Paraíso'. A page number in **bold type** indicates a photograph; a page number in *italic type* indicates a map reference. Bus numbers, *not* page references, follow the 🚌-symbol. See bus timetables pages 126-132.

Achada do Teixeira 15, *16-17*, 23-4, 89-90, 93, 98
Águas Mansas 18, *71*, 74 🚌 77
Apresentação *56*, *57*, 111
Arco da Calheta 33 🚌 107
Arco de São Jorge 29 🚌 103
Assomada 14, **18-19**, 67-8, *71* 🚌 2, 20, 23, 53, 78, 113
Babosas 13, 29, 63, **64**, 69, 70 🚌 22
Baía da Abra 15, **21**, 75-6, 77
Balcões 15, *16-17*, 25, **29**, 95, 99
Barreiras 58, *59*, 62 🚌 4, 6, 7, 107
Bica da Cana *16-17*, 110
Boa Morte 13, 58, *59*, **61** 🚌 148
Boaventura 27-8, 93 🚌 6, 103
Boca da Corrida 13, 52, *54*
Boca do Cerro *16-17*, 53, 55
Boca do Risco 78, 80, *81*, **82-3**, 85
Boca dos Corgos *16-17*, *54*
Boca dos Namorados 51, *54*
Boqueirão 14 🚌 60
Cabo Garajau 18, 20, 26
Cabo Girão 21-2, 27, *59* 🚌 154
Caldeira *59*, 60
Caldeirão Verde *16-17*, 88, 95
Calheta 33 🚌 107
Camacha 18, 63, 66-7, 69-70, *71*, 72-3, 99 🚌 29, 77
Câmara de Lobos 21, 27, 43, *45* 🚌 1, 4, 6, 7, 96, 107, 154
Campanário 27, 58, *59*, 60 🚌 4, 6, 7, 107
Campo Grande *16-17*, **114-5**, *120*, 122
Cancela 20
Candelária *56* 🚌 4, 107
Canhas 32-3, 114, 122, 125 🚌 107
Caniçal 75-6, 77, 81 🚌 113
Caniço 20, 26 🚌 2, 23, 25, 53, 78, 113, 136, 155
Caramujo *16-17*, 108, 110
Casa do Elias (Quebradas) 31

Cascalho *16-17*, 106, **107**
Chão dos Louros *16-17*, 27 🚌 6
Chamorra 44, *45*, 50 🚌 8, 9
Choupana 69, *70*
Corticeiras 52, *54*, *59* 🚌 96
Corujeira *56*, 57
Cova da Roda 15, *16-17*, 24, 29, **86**, 90, 94
Cova das Pedras *80*
Cruzinhas *16-17*, 25, 94, 95 🚌 103
Curral das Freiras *16-17*, 21, 22, 44, *45*, **50**, 53, *54*, 55, 91, 93 🚌 81
Curral de Baixo *45*, 46, 51, *54*
Curral dos Romeiros 13, 29, 63, **64**, *70* 🚌 22, 30
Eira de Fora 18, *71*, 73-4 🚌 77
Eira do Serrado 21, **22**, *45*, 54
Encumeada *16-17*, **26**, 27, 52, 55, 89, **92**, 101, 105-6, 108, 110-11 🚌 6
Espigão Amarelo *81*, 82-3, 85
Estanquinhos *16-17*
Estreito da Calheta 33 🚌 107
Estreito de Câmara de Lobos 22, 52, 58, *59* 🚌 4, 6, 7, 96, 107, 154
Faial 23-5, 27, 94 🚌 53, 78, 103
Fajã 44, *45*, 48, *54*
Fajã da Noguera *16-17*, 95
Fajã das Galinhas *45*, 48, *54*
Fajã de Dentro *45*, 48
Fajã do Penedo *16-17*, 93 🚌 103
Fajã dos Cardos *16-17*, 91, 93
Fanal **31**, *120-2*, **123**
Feiteiras *16-17*, 101, 104, 108 🚌 6
Fenda do Ferreiro *16-17*, 54
Florenças 117, *118* 🚌 107
Folhadal *16-17*, 101, 103
Fonte do Bispo 31
Garachico *59*, 60 🚌 4, 6, 7, 96, 107, 154
Gaula 63, 66, 68, *71* 🚌 60
Ginjas *16-17*, 101, 103, **107**, 108, 110

Homem em Pé 15, *16-17*, 24, **88**, 90, 98
Jardim Botánico 🚌 30
Jardim da Serra 13, 22, 52, *54*
Jardim do Mar *113*
João Frino 71, 72, **74** 🚌 77
Lamaceiros 16, *71*, 74, 99-100
Lapa do Galho *16-17*, 16, **26**, 101
Levada
  Calheta—Ponta do Pargo **32**, *113*, 114, 117, 118-*19*
  da Central da Ribeira da Janela *120*, 123
  da Portela *71*, *80*, 99, 100
  da Serra (Bica da Cana) 16-17, **109**, 110
  da Serra (Santo da Serra) 14, 26, 69, *70-1*, 72, **74**
  das Rabaças *16-17*, **100**, 106, 108
  das Vinte e Cinco Fontes 117, *119*, **119**, *120*, 125
  do Caldeirão Verde *16-17*, 87, **88**, 90
  do Caniço 66, 68, *71*
  do Curral e Castelejo 44, *45*, **46-7**, *54*, 93
  do Furado *16-17*, *70*, 95, **98**, 99
  do Lombo do Mouro *16-17*, *56*, 108, 110-**11**
  do Norte 13, 16, *16-17*, **55**, 58, *59*, **61**, **92**, 101, 105-6, 110
  do Paúl **114-15**, *119*, *120*, 122
  do Risco *119*, *120*, 124-5
  dos Piornais 13, 42, *45*, *54*
  dos Tornos 14, 63, **64**, **65**, 69, *70-1*, **75**
  Machico—Caniçal *71*, *78*, *80-1*, **84**
  Nova (Tábua) *56*
Lombada 13, 43, *45* 🚌 1, 3
Lombada da Ponta do Sol 33
Lombo do Galego *16-17*, 94-5
Lombo do Mouro *16-17*, **111**
Lombo Grande 63, 66, *71*, 93 🚌 60
Loreto 114, 117, *118* 🚌 107
Machico 18-19, *78*, *81* 🚌 20, 23, 53, 78, 113
Madelena do Mar 33 🚌 4
Maroços 79, *80*
Matur 20 🚌 23, 25, 53, 113
Miradouro do Juncal *16-17*, 23
Monte 13, 27, 29, 63, **64**, 69, *70*, 72 🚌 20, 21, 103
Nogueira 66, *71*
Palheiro Ferreiro 18, **20**, 63, 65, *70* 🚌 29, 30, 77
Passo de Ares *16-17*, 53, *54*
Paúl da Serra *16-17*, 30, **31**, 32-3, **109**, **111**, **113**, **114-15**, *120*, 121-2
Paúl do Mar **112**, *113*

Penha de Águia 25, *80*, **86**, 95
Pico
  do Arieiro 15, *16-17*, 23, 29, 89, 94, 96, **97**, **111**
  das Pedras *16-17*, 24, 29, 87, 90, 94
  das Torres *16-17*, **29**, 93, 97, **111**
  do Facho 15, 19, 78, *81*
  do Gato *16-17*, **29**, 93, 97, **111**
  dos Barcelos 21, *45* 🚌 8, 9
  Grande *16-17*, 52, **53**, 55, **102**, **111**
  Redondo 16, *16-17*, **104**, 105
  Ruivo *16-17*, 24, **29**, 89-90, 93, 96, 98, **111**
Pináculo *16-17*, 108, 110
Poiso *16-17*, 23, 26-7, 29 🚌 103
Ponta da Oliveira 🚌 155
Ponta das Gaivotas 76, 77
Ponta Delgada 28 🚌 6
Ponta de São Lourenço 18-19, **21**, 75, **76**, 77
Ponta do Pargo 33 🚌 107, 150
Ponta do Sol 33 🚌 4, 107
Portela 23-4, *71*, 72, 78, *80*, 99-100 🚌 53
Porto da Cruz 23, **24**, *80*, 82-3, 86 🚌 53, 78
Porto Moniz 30, 31, *120* 🚌 150
Praínha 75, 77
Prazeres 16, 33, **112**, *113*, **113** 🚌 107
Preces *45* 🚌 8, 9
Quebradas (Funchal) 43, *45* 🚌 2
Quebradas (Paúl da Serra) 31
Queimadas 15, *16-17*, 24, 29, **86**, 87-8, 94, 96, 98
Quinta Grande 27, 58, *59*, 60 🚌 4, 6, 7, 107
Rabaçal 16, 114, **116-17**, *119*, **119**, *120*
Raposeira **32**, 33 🚌 107
Ribeira
  da Boaventura *71*, 74
  Brava 13, **26**, *56*, *59*, **62**, 91
  da Calheta *118*, **119**
  da Janela 30, 31, 33, *120*
  da Metade *16-17*, 23, 90
  da Tábua **55**, *56*
  de Machico *71*, **78**, 79, *80*, *81*
  do Curral *45*, 46, 51, *54*, 93
  do Porto Novo 14, **62**, 66, **67**, *71*, 73, **75**
  dos Socorridos 13, 42, **43**, *45*, 49
  Sêca (Faial) *16-17*, 95
  Sêca (Machico) 79, *81*, 82-4
Ribeira Brava **26**, 27, 30, 33, *56*, *59*, **62**, 111 🚌 4, 6, 7, 107

Ribeira da Janela *120*, 121, 123 🚌 150
Ribeira de Machico *71*, 78, *80* 🚌 53
Ribeira Sêca 79, *81*, 82-4 🚌 113
Ribeiro Frio *16-17*, 24, 25, 29, 99 🚌 103
Ribeirinha 66, *71*
Risco 117, **118**, *119*, *120*, 124
Rochão *70*, 73
Romeiros 63, 64, *70*
Rosário *16-17*, 27 🚌 6
Salgados 67, 68, *71*
Santa 31 🚌 150
Santa Cruz 18, 20 🚌 9, 23, 25, 113
Santana *16-17*, 23-4, 27, 29, 87, 88, 89, 96, 98 🚌 103
Santo Amaro *45*, 50 🚌 8, 9
Santo da Serra 18-19, *71*, **72-3**, 74, *80* 🚌 20, 25, 77, 78

São Jorge 29, 88 🚌 103
São Martinho *45*, **49** 🚌 2, 8, 9
São Roque do Faial *16-17*, **86**
São Vicente *16-17*, 27-8, 30 🚌 6, 150
Seixal 30, *120* 🚌 150
Serra de Água *16-17*, **26**, 27, 55, 62 🚌 6
Sitio das Quatro Estradas *71*, 72, 74 🚌 77
Tábua 33, **55**, *56* 🚌 4, 107
Terreiro da Luta 23, 69, *70* 🚌 103
Torrinhas *16-17*, 89, 92, 93
Valé do Paraíso 14, 26, **68**, 69, *70* 🚌 29, 77
Vinháticos, Pousada dos *16-17*, 27, **28**, 36, 55, 105 🚌 6
Vinte e Cinco Fontes *119*, **119**, *120*, 124
Vitória 13, 42, 43, *45* 🚌 1, 4, 6, 7, 27, 50, 96, 107, 154

Pronunciation/translation of some index entries

achada (ah-sháh-dah) small plateau
água (áh-gwah) water
arco (áhr-koh) arc or curving mountain ridge
baía (bah-ée-ah) bay
balcões (bahl-kóyngs) balconies
baixo (bŷe-joh) lower
bica (bée-kah) small spring
boca (bóh-kah) mountain pass (literally 'mouth')
brava (bráh-vah) wild
cabo (káh-boh) cape
caldeirão (kahl-day-roúngh) cauldron, crater, basin
calheta (cahl-yéy-tah) creek
câmara (káh-mah-rah) chamber
campo (káhm-poh) plain
caniço (kah-née-soh) reed
chão (shoúng) flat place
choupana (show-páh-nah) cottage
corticeiras (kohr-tee-sáy-rahs) small cork trees
cova (kóh-vah) pit, cave
cruzinhas (kru-zéen-yahs) crossroads

dentro (déhn-troh) inside
eira (ẽye-rah) threshing floor
encumeada (in-koo-mee-áh-dah) summit with good views
estanquinhos (esh-tahn-kéen-yohs) small ponds
estreito (esh-tráy-toh) the straights above
faial (fai-áhl) beech grove
fajã (fah-jáh) small landslip
fonte (fóhn-tay) spring
fora (fóh-rah) outside
gaula (gáow-lah) gaulish
ginja (géen-jah) cherry
janela (jha-néh-lah) window
jardim (jahr-déengh) garden
lamaceiros (lah-mah-sáy-roos) marshy place
lombo (lóh-moh) ridge separating two parallel ravines
monte (móhn-teh) mount
mouro (móoh-roh) moorish
nogueira (noh-gáy-rah) nut tree
palheiro (pahl-yéh-roh) thatched cottage

paúl (pah-óol) marshland
penha (péyn-yah) rock
pico (pée-koh) peak
poio (póy-oh) terrace
poiso (póy-soh) pause
ponta (póhn-tah) point
portela (pohr-téh-lah) little gateway
porto (póhr-toh) port
praínha (prah-éen-yah) small beach
prazer (prah-zéhr) pleasure
quebrada (kay-bráh-dah) steep slope
queimada (kay-máh-dah) burnt
rabaça (rah-báh-zah) wild celery
ribeira (ree-báy-rah) river or river valley
risco (réesh-koh) danger
seixal (sáy-shal) pebbly place
serra (séh-rah) mountain range
sitio (sée-tee-oh) place
torrinhas (toh-réen-yahs) turrets
vinháticos (veen-yáh-tee-kohs) indigenous laurels

STOP PRESS — AUTUMN 1991

CAR TOURS: Much of the Funchal ring road is now open. The EN204 between the Paúl da Serra and Encumeada, and the EN213 from Madalena to Calheta should be open in 1992.

WHERE TO STAY

Rest houses: Book these *in writing, well in advance of your visit.* For the **Pico Ruivo** rest house, write to the Tourist Office, Avenida Arriaga, 9000 Funchal. For the government rest houses at **Rabaçal** and **Queimadas**, write to the Gabinete do Presidente, Quinta Vigia, 9000 Funchal. In both cases state the house in which accommodation is required, number of nights, number of persons. You can also book during your visit (note that Quinta Vigia is no. 13 on our town plan), but the government rest houses are likely to be fully booked. All rest houses provide bedding and cooking facilities. Take your own provisions and remember that all are in the mountains, there is no heating except for open fires, and you will need to take plenty of warm clothing. Note also that it *may* be possible to stay at some **forestry houses** (Pico das Pedras, etc). Enquire on booking.

Camping: There is only one 'official' site, at **Porto Moniz.** You can pitch a tent at Pico das Pedras and Queimadas also, and it's likely that one of the keepers will let you use a shower/toilet. Backpacking is *not* encouraged for several reasons, including the danger of fires.

Hotels: There are now hotels at Ribeira Brava, Porto Moniz, Santana and São Vicente. The *pousada* at Arieiro is open. Details from your tour operator or the Portuguese Tourist Office.

WALKS (and their corresponding picnics)

Walk 1: *To start the walk,* climb the hill past the Quinta do Sol Hotel. Turn left into the Camino da Casa Branca and right up the Ladeira da Casa Branca. By the stadium you come to the wide Rua dos Estados Unidos; the levada is on the left of this road, down some steps. The walk is further interrupted by the new ring road in a few places, but the levada is easily regained. **Important: This walk ends at the viewpoint shown on page 43.** *Do* go a few paces beyond it to *look* at the tunnels, but please do not attempt to go through them!

Walk 2: We stress that the *main walk is only for experts* and often *impassable* due to landslides. Roadworks at Curral have altered the start of the walk. Ask in the village how to get down to the levada. The levada above Fajã was repaired in 1991 and is now passable (but wet; it passes under a waterfall!). If you are doing the *Alternative walk* (suitable for everyone), you may encounter roadworks in the area of São Martinho Church. Ask for 'le-**vah**-dah **pah**-rah Sha-**more**-ah' (the levada to Chamora) and someone will point the way. The *Short walk* is no longer possible because of roadworks; instead, why not try a shorter version of the Alternative walk.

Walk 3: Forest fires badly damaged this route, which was being repaired in 1991. *Extreme caution* is recommended; the way may still be scree-covered and vertiginous. If the telephone poles at the Boca dos Namorados are not replaced, turn left on the wide track at the pass and then be sure to *fork right immediately* on a narrow path. *Grade: strenuous; potentially hazardous.*

Walk 4: There are *no* taxis at Corticeiras, but the owner of the bar by the bus stop can call one for you (from Estreito). If you are walking to Boca da Corrida from Corticeiras, continue straight ahead from the bus stop (do *not* go sharply downhill to the left). The road is level at first and then goes downhill. When it turns sharp left, bear right and reach the Central da Pareira in 8min. From here climb to the pass. At any time roadworks may interrupt this walk in the valley of the Ribeira do Poço. At press date roadworks had stopped at the pipe (10min from the EN104). If roadworks make the walk impassable east of the pipe, return to the path passed at 4h15min (15min east of the bridge). This is a *very clear* path at the start. Twenty minutes down, go right at a fork. Fifteen minutes later, when a path goes back to the right, continue straight on. Now the going gets *very steep;* your goal is the bridge far below, and you drop down to it in fifteen minutes. Just before reaching the bridge, the path deteriorates so badly that you risk turning an ankle; a walking stick helps with this 15ft descent. After crossing the bridge, climb up to the electricity poles ahead, where you find a narrow levada. Follow it to the left and take the first steps off (right), to climb to the higher electricity poles, which are on the wide Levada do Norte (15min from the bridge). Turn left and reach the power station in 15min; from there it's 30min up to Vinháticos.

Walk 5: This levada has been in use again since 1990, and some people will find the walk too vertiginous, since it will not be possible to walk in the levada channel.

Walk 8: The bus stop has been moved to the *east* of the church.

Walk 10: The levada is now empty all the way to the Santo da Serra waterhouse.

Walk 11: We urge you to take a taxi to the viewpoint at the end of the EN101-3 to start the walk.

Walk 13: There is now a *tarred* road all round the Ribeira Sêca valley, and the bus stop is now *east* of the Ribeira Sêca road. *To start out,* walk a few metres *back* the way the bus came and then uphill on a *tarred* road on your *right.* Follow the road to the 'top', where it makes a narrow U-turn in the valley. Just before the U-turn, concrete steps at the right of an electric pole lead up to the levada; it takes about 15min to climb from this point up to the levada, which you join just beyond the last (highest) electricity pole. There may be some changes at the end of the walk, but your destination is clearly visible.

Walk 14: Many railings are in *poor condition,* and the walk is *only safe for very sure-footed walkers with no fear of vertigo.*

Walk 15: This walk may be interrupted by roadworks near Torrinhas. Enquire at the Pico Ruivo rest house (or at the bar at Encumeada, if you are doing the walk in reverse) before setting out.

Walk 16: This walk may be interrupted by roadworks. Enquire at the Pico Ruivo rest house (or in Curral das Freiras, if you are doing the walk in reverse) before setting out. Moreover, this path has not been maintained in the last two years, and *we no longer recommend this walk.*

Walk 17: The *times* given for this walk are too long; moreover the walk is moderate, *not* strenuous. *The entire walk takes only 2h35min.*

Walk 19: There is an error on the map. The bus symbol should be on the *EN101* at Portela, *not* on the EN102. There is a pleasant café/bar at the start of the walk (Victor's).

Walks 20-22: Work is going on to widen the Levada do Norte. It is not possible to go beyond the tunnel to Cascalho (**Walk 22**). Most of the time the levada path will be accessible, but you may be turned back, if blasting is going on. A fire has made route-finding on **Walk 21** very difficult.

Walk 23: The path up to the Levada do Lombo do Mouro is obliterated. Follow the new road west, until you come to where the levada crosses the road (about 1h—1h15min). Here turn right and follow the levada northeast, until you reach the path (on your left) up to the Levada da Serra.

Walk 24: Only *experts equipped with walking boots* should attempt this walk. You must *scramble over huge rocks and boulders straight down* a buttress to the levada (some 15min beyond where the levada crosses the new road). Once on the levada, several scree areas must be crossed — vertiginous, but perfectly safe. Allow about 6 hours for the walk, not five.